MVFOL

The Contender

and Related Readings

McDougal Littell
A HOUGHTON MIFFLIN COMPANY
Evanston, Illinois   Boston   Dallas

Acknowledgments

HarperCollins Publishers, Inc.: *The Contender* by Robert Lipsyte. Copyright © 1967 by Robert Lipsyte. Reprinted by permission of HarperCollins Publishers, Inc.

The Estate of James Merrill: "The Seventh Round" by James Merrill. Originally appeared in *The Yellow Pages* (1974). Reprinted by permission of J. D. McClatchy, Literary Executor for the Estate of James Merrill.

Dell Books: "Fury" by T. Ernesto Bethancourt, from *Ultimate Sports*, edited by Donald R. Gallo. Copyright © 1995 by T. Ernesto Bethancourt. Used by permission of Dell Books, a division of Bantam Doubleday Dell Publishing Group, Inc.

Murray Pollinger, Literary Agent: "A Crown of Wild Olive" by Rosemary Sutcliff, from *Heather, Oak and Olive*, first published in North America by E. P. Dutton. Reprinted by permission of Murray Pollinger, Literary Agent.

HarperCollins Publishers, Inc.: Excerpt from *Black Boy* by Richard Wright. Copyright 1945 by Richard Wright. Copyright renewed 1973 by Ellen Wright. Reprinted by permission of HarperCollins Publishers, Inc.

Continued on page 246

Cover illustration by Michael Steirnagle.

ISBN 0-395-83358-2

56789--QNT--03 02 01 00 99

Contents

The Contender

Robert Lipsyte

Chapter 1

He waited on the stoop until twilight, pretending to watch the sun melt into the dirty gray Harlem sky. Up and down the street transistor radios clicked on and hummed into the sour air. Men dragged out card tables, laughing. Cars cruised through the garbage and broken glass, older guys showing off their Friday night girls. Another five minutes, he thought. I'll give James another five minutes.

"You still here, Alfred?" Aunt Pearl came out on the stoop, her round face damp from the kitchen.

He tried to sound casual. "You know James. He better hurry or we'll miss the first picture."

"He's never been this late, Alfred. Why don't you go upstairs and call his house? Maybe he's sick."

"James ain't sick." Alfred stood up.

"How you know that?" Her eyes narrowed. "You know where he's at?"

"Maybe."

"He's hangin' out with those worthless punks, ain't he, Alfred? Maybe you just better . . . Alfred!"

But he was already off the stoop and moving fast, his sneakers slapping on the sidewalk. Packs of little kids, raggedy and skinny, raced past him along the gutter's edge, kicking empty beer cans ahead of them. Used to do that too, when we were little, he thought. One thing I could always do better than James. I was always faster. Big deal. He slowed down.

He stopped at the mouth of the alley, and took a deep breath. What am I, James' shadow or something? I don't need him. But he marched to the basement steps, and plunged down into the clubroom.

Hollis and Sonny were sprawled on the long, sagging couch, snapping their fingers to a scratchy record. Major was flexing his arm muscles at the cracked mirror over the mop sink. Only James, trying to read a magazine in the dim light of the naked bulb, looked up.

"Hey, man, what's happening?"

"Nothing much," said Alfred. "Ready to go to the movies?"

"Not unless it's free night," said James.

"I got some money," said Alfred.

Major turned slowly and let his muscles relax. "How much you got, Alfred?"

Sonny and Hollis stopped snapping.

"I said, 'How much you got, Alfred?'"

"Nothing," mumbled Alfred, staring down at the tips of his sneakers.

"You the only one workin', and you got paid today," said Major. "What you got?"

"Gave it to my aunt," said Alfred.

"'Gave it to my aunt,'" mimicked Major. "You such a good sweet boy. Old Uncle Alfred."

Sonny giggled, and Hollis grinned, buck-toothed. James looked away.

"Don't you know this club has got dues?" Major folded his arms across his bulging T-shirt.

Hollis leaned back in the couch. "Go collect the dues, Sonny. Turn Alfred upside down and make the dues fall out his pocket."

"'Turn Alfred upside down,'" echoed Sonny, blankly. He stood up, taller than any of them and almost as heavily muscled as Major. "Upside down."

"Hold on," said James. "Alfred's my guest. I invited him to come down."

Alfred took a step backward, nearly knocking over

an old wooden chair. "Let's go, James."

Major swaggered across the room, the metal tips on his pointed shoes clicking on the concrete floor. "How much them Jews give you for slavin', Uncle Alfred?"

"Jews squeeze the eagle till it screams," said Hollis. "The eagle screams, 'Faster, Alfred, sweep that floor, you skinny nigger.'"

"They been all right to me," said Alfred.

"How come you ain't workin' right now?" said Major, circling until he stood between Alfred and the door.

"Grocery's closed."

"At eight o'clock?"

"They close early on Friday to go to synagogue."

"They go pray for more dollars," said Hollis. Even James smiled.

"No," said Alfred. "The Epsteins are very religious. They don't even touch money after sundown on Fridays."

"That's a lie," said Major.

"No. They even leave money in the cash register so they won't have to . . ." He bit his lip. Water dripped into the mop sink, small explosions in the suddenly silent room.

"Let's get it," whispered Hollis.

"Show us," said Major.

"No, I—"

"You just a slave," sneered Major. "You was born a slave. You gonna die a slave."

"'Slave,'" echoed Sonny.

"I see you now, boy, old and stooped," said Major, shuffling to the center of the room. "Old and stooped. You be scratching your head and saying, 'Yassuh, Mistuh Lou, lemme brush them hairs offen your coat; yassuh, Mistuh Jake, I be pleased iffen you 'low me to wash your car.'"

Sonny and Hollis began to laugh as Major shuffled around the dim, warm room, his muscular arms dangling like a monkey's, his eyes rolling, his black head bobbing in ugly imitation of an old-time Negro servant. "I can see you now, Alfred, good old Uncle Alfred. 'Yassuh, Mistuh Ben, I be so grat-i-fied iffen you'd kick me now and again, show how much you white folks love us.'"

The laughter rose, high-pitched and nervous. Alfred peeked at their faces, black and sweating in the semi-circle around him. Hollis and Sonny, grinning and nodding. James' chubby face was set and unsmiling as Major continued his imitation, scratching his nose, pouting his lips, and shambling loosely like a puppet at the end of jerking strings.

Alfred's hands were wet.

"You come on with us," said James. "You know just where to—"

"We don't need him if he's scared," said Hollis.

"He isn't scared, not him," said James. "Look, Alfred, you don't owe them anything."

"They gave me a job," said Alfred, surprised at how far away his own voice sounded.

"Big job," said Hollis.

"Yassuh," yelled Major, shuffling back into the center. "'Mistuh Lou, I been sweepin' out your store forty year now, how 'bout lettin' me de-li-ver groceries on the bi-cy-cle oncet in a while?'"

Alfred swallowed hard. "They was the only ones gave me a job when I quit school," he yelled.

They fell quiet again.

"You come on, Alfred," said James, softly. "Whitey been stealing from us for three hundred years. We just going to take some back."

"No."

"You could stay outside, be lookout," said James.

Major shouldered in between them. "You coming?"

Alfred shook his head.

"Let's go," said Major, moving toward the door. He turned at the first step, Sonny and Hollis at his heels. "James?"

"Let's go to the movies, James," said Alfred.

"That's all you ever want to do," said James.

They stared at each other.

"You coming, James, or you gonna be a slave too?"

James turned away. He followed the others up the steps to the street. The door banged shut behind them. Fool, thought Alfred. Had to open your mouth. He kicked the chair across the room.

"Good kick, man. Where's everybody going in such a hurry?" Henry limped down into the clubroom, dragging his crippled left leg, the perpetual grin spread across his skinny face.

Alfred shrugged.

"Play some cards?"

"I gotta go, Henry."

"Hey, Alfred, you know what I'm doing now? Mr. Donatelli, the fight manager, he's letting me . . . Where you going?"

"Out."

The stench of wine and garbage still hung in the moist June air. He jammed his hands into the pockets of his tight blue slacks, watching the cars cruise past. Another year, he thought, be eighteen, able to drive. Sure. On grocery-boy pay. Slave. The bells of the ice cream truck jangled across the street, and a sudden roar burst from a dozen transistor radios. Somebody must have hit a home run. The Epsteins would be in their synagogue now, wearing skull caps and praying.

He started to walk toward his house, then stopped. Aunt Pearl would be sitting on the stoop, waving the fan the undertaker gave away at summer funerals. She would ask him why he wasn't with James. She would know if he was lying. He went back down to the clubroom.

Henry was punching at his reflection in the cracked mirror. He dropped his hands when he saw Alfred, and the big grin turned sheepish.

"Shadowboxing," he said.

"Yeah."

"Mr. Donatelli's letting me work around the gym, take care of the gloves and wash the mouthpieces."

"Big job."

"You ought to come up, Alfred. Willie Streeter's training now. He's going to fight in Madison Square Garden next week."

"Yeah."

"Lotta guys come up and train," said Henry.

"Yeah."

"Hey, man, where you—"

Out on the street again, he idly watched a green-and-white police cruiser slide by, a thick, hairy white arm hanging out of the open window. Alfred stiffened. The burglar alarm, the new silent burglar alarm installed at Epsteins' the other night. How could I forget about that? They'd never hear it go off. It would ring in the detectives' office, and they'd call the police right away. He began to run. Got to get to James, got to tell James. But the radio inside the police car began to crackle and sputter, as if it had read his mind. The car suddenly picked up speed.

Silently, a second police car joined the first. Then both wheeled around the corner, roaring into noise and light, motors growling, headlights glaring, sirens howling. Alfred slowed down as hundreds of people came off stoops and street corners, and poured out of bars toward four cruisers parked behind Epsteins'. The doors of the police cars were open, and the red roof lights were blinking.

He heard shouts, and a voice yelled, "Stop, stop." A shot rang out. The warning shot.

He started running again, toward the shot, but the crowd thickened in front of him. "They caught one," someone yelled from an upstairs window. The crowd surged forward, sweeping Alfred along. He tried to push through, but the crowd was too tightly packed.

"The Man," mumbled a voice off to his left. "Always lookin' to put his foot on a black throat."

"You sayin' the truth, brother."

"Only reason po-lice up here to watch out for them white stores."

"So right."

Police car doors slammed shut, and the cruisers drove away, their sirens on. The crowd began to drift back to their stoops, to the drinks they had left on bars. Alfred passed an old man who lived in his building, and grabbed his arm.

"You see who they caught?"

The old man shook his head. "They hustled him away too fast."

"Just one?"

"A couple got away."

Alfred pushed his way out of the crowd, and onto a side street. He had to think. The three who got away would split up and hide. If James made it, there would be only one place for him to go. Alfred circled toward the park, his hands in his pockets, his head low. He kept his feet moving slowly. Police cars cruised by, and he felt eyes staring out at him. Keep walking slow.

It was quiet in the park. Couples were drinking

and whispering on the grass, and the transistors were turned down. He saw the rock, big as a truck, outlined against a purple-black sky, and his feet moved faster, over the small rocks, over the low thicket of bushes. He dropped to his knees and wriggled through the tangle of stunted, twisted trees that hid the opening beneath the huge rock. On his elbows, he crawled into the cave.

He had forgotten how small it was. He could barely sit up. The thin layer of loose dirt on the flat rock floor was cool against his palms, and his head touched the jagged rock ceiling. He drew his knees up to his chest, and held them. He slowed his breathing, and strained his ears for James.

He tried to remember the first time he had been in the cave. Ten years ago. James was there, too. He was hardly ever in the cave without James—Alfred squeezed against the back, James up front, poking out his head to see if the coast was clear. They were just little kids then, running away from older boys, like Major, who tried to hold them up for nickels on the street. They'd break and run when they saw Major coming, circle around till they were out of sight, then sprint into the park. They'd scramble through the underbrush into the cave, shaking and out of breath, clapping their hands over each other's mouths to muffle their laughter. After a while, James might start his imitations. He would be Mrs. McCormick, their public school principal, pressing his lips together until they almost disappeared, fluttering his eyelids. "Chil-dren. With-out ed-u-ca-tion man is a sav-age beast." They'd collapse into hiccuping laughter.

And then James might screw up his face and make his eyes bulge, like Rick, the white college boy who ran the summer program. "Gotta hang in there, guys.

Can't lose if you hang in there." They liked Rick, who showed them how professional basketball players took foul shots, and how to throw curve balls. They were getting good too, until Major and Sonny and Hollis began hanging around the playground, making remarks and kicking balls out of their hands. One summer Rick just didn't come back.

A twig snapped outside.

"James?" he whispered.

There was a soft, scampering sound, then quiet again. Squirrel.

James had found the cave the summer they were rock hunting. James had a library book on rocks, and they spent days just wandering around the park, filling their pockets with little rocks that matched the pictures in the book. For a while they kept their rocks in the cave, and then James took them home. He was going to arrange them in a cardboard box and bring them to school in September. James' father came home drunk one night and dropped all the rocks down the air shaft.

Far away, a police siren whined. Alfred shivered. C'mon, James, make it, man, get away. He moved his head, and dirt fell off the ceiling of the cave into his eyes and mouth.

He remembered the night his own father left home forever. He was ten. James sat with him then, in the cave. They talked, and it made him feel a little better. And James was there three years later when Alfred's mother died of pneumonia in the city hospital, sitting with him all night, whispering, "Gonna be all right, Alfred. I'm gonna stick by you. We're partners, right?" Then they crawled out of the cave, and James walked him back to his new home with Aunt Pearl and her three little daughters.

C'mon, James, where are you? Alfred's legs began

to cramp and stiffen. Tears streamed down his cheeks.

James tried to talk him into staying in school. "Can't get a good job without that piece of paper, Alfred." James was going to be an engineer, and build things. Alfred could help him. They'd make a fortune and drive back to the neighborhood in a white Cadillac, and go right to the cave, crawl on the ground in their silk suits, and pull out any little kids they found in there and buy them something really fine. Never happen now. I quit school, and after all that talk, James quits four months later.

He pinched his calves to stop his legs from falling asleep. Five minutes, give him another five minutes.

James didn't even look for a job, started hanging around with Major and Hollis, believing them when they said the white man would never let him build anything but garbage heaps. He started going to the clubroom in the basement of the building where Henry's father was superintendent. Maybe the partnership started busting up then. If only James had come to the movies tonight, like every other Friday night. And that burglar alarm—how could I forget about that burglar alarm?

He moved his head again, and tasted more dirt. Maybe the police caught James. Or maybe he got away, and had a better place to hide now. With Major.

Slowly, he crawled out.

It was pitch-dark. The big rock was hard to see against the black sky. The transistors were silent. He crept carefully, until no one who might be watching could tell where he had come from. Then he stood up and walked toward home. The side streets were quieter now. His legs began to lose their stiffness. He turned down his street.

"Why it's good old Uncle Alfred."

He froze. Major's arms were folded across his chest, and Hollis' lips were pulled back in a bucktoothed grin.

"Where's James?"

"'Where's James?'" mimicked Major.

"They caught him, you . . ." snarled Hollis, pushing Sonny toward Alfred, and then the four of them were in a tight pile of swinging arms and legs, kicking, cuffing, punching, and Alfred smashed into the pavement, under Sonny, and the elbows and fists began crashing into his sides, his head, his stomach.

"You knew 'bout that alarm," grunted Major, hammering down on him.

"I forgot, I would of . . ." Alfred tasted his own blood, warm and salty, and he felt the pavement scrape the skin off his shoulder blades. He struggled, trying to kick upwards, but the three of them were too much, bearing down, slugging, stomping . . .

"Split," hissed Major, and they were standing. "We'll get you . . ." and they were gone.

Far down the block, two patrolmen, one black, one white, walked lightly, looking over each other's shoulders, glancing up at the rooftops. Alfred dragged himself into an alley, and crawled painfully behind a garbage can. He swallowed back his nausea as a rat scurried over his arm, squealing. The two policemen whirled at the sound, hands on their guns. They looked at each other, shrugged, and walked on. Alfred fainted.

Chapter 2

He woke up in his aunt's bed, blinking against the white glare of the morning sun. He felt her calloused hand move gently over his swollen jaw long before he saw her red-rimmed eyes peering down at him.

"How do you feel, Alfred, honey?" Her voice, usually so warm and light, sounded husky and tired.

"I'm okay, Aunt Pearl."

"Thank the Lord." She lowered herself to the edge of the narrow bed. "We was so scared for you, Alfred. Prayed all night, prayed to God and to your sweet momma, rest her soul, got right down on—"

"It's okay, Aunt Pearl, I'm okay." He moved his legs under the sheet, then his arms. Numb, aching pain everywhere, but everything moving, nothing broken.

"What happened, Alfred? When Henry and Mister Johnson carried you—"

"Henry?"

"He found you. You was wandering around with your eyes shut, and he went and got his daddy to help carry you home. What happened, Alfred?"

"The, uh, old stone fence off Lenox, Aunt Pearl. I was walking on it, and . . . a . . . a big dog jumped up. Knocked me off."

"Uh, huh," she said, but he could see by her eyes she knew he was lying. She turned, and he saw his three little cousins jammed in the doorway, staring at him. "You heard what happened, now you go out and play. Go ahead, give Alfred a chance to rest. Charlene, you be sure you're all back for supper. Mrs.

Elversen's havin' a party, and I'll be bringin' home all kinds of good things."

The twins began to edge back, but Charlene kept staring. It seemed to Alfred that her eyes were red-rimmed, too. "Go on, now."

Aunt Pearl waited until they had clattered out of the apartment and down the tenement stairs before she turned back to Alfred. She was frowning. "James was arrested last night, Alfred. For trying to break into Epsteins'."

"I know."

"You knew about it, him going?"

"Yes."

"But you wasn't with him, that right?"

"That's right."

"He wanted you to go, that right?"

When he didn't answer, she leaned closer. "Who beat you, Alfred?"

"I fell off the fence."

She shook her head, her hands again on his aching face. "Oh, Alfred, it's like you're my own son. I know you try so hard, you so good. I know it ain't easy, living here. Someday, someday we're gonna move away, Alfred, and we . . ." She began to cry, softly.

After a while she rose and smoothed the front of her cotton dress. "I got to work now, Alfred. Be back about eight tonight. You rest. There's some food by the bed, you eat something right now."

She paused at the door, and forced a smile. Weakly, he waved back, and slipped again into sleep.

It was noon when he awoke again. His head felt clear. The pain in his arms and legs seemed to have eased. Biting carefully on aching teeth, he ate the bread and cheese and baloney she had left by the bed, and drank some of the milk, now warm. Street sounds floated up through the open window, children yelling, the thud of a rubber ball against the pavement, four voices singing, "Hey, bay-bee, you're num-ber one, you're . . . ," cars honking Saturday strollers out of their way. Far off, he heard a police siren knife through the street noise. He felt it in his belly.

James was in jail. He burrowed deeper into the bed. It was his fault, letting it slip about the money in the cash register. His fault again for not remembering about the new burglar alarm. Nice bed, soft and safe, away from all of them, he thought. Major and Hollis out on the street, looking to get me. The Epsteins, they'll be asking questions on Monday morning. They know James is my best friend. *Was* my best friend. No partner, nothing. Stay in bed, man, curl up like a baby, close your eyes, make the world go away. The big white world full of cans to stack and floors to sweep and pails of garbage to drag out back. Big job. Maybe James was right to try to get some of that money, only wrong to get caught. Just stay in bed, man, until you're eighteen, then join the Army. No, stay in bed forever.

He made himself get up then, pushing his long, wiry legs over the edge of the bed, standing on the little throw rug until the quivering stopped. He went into the bathroom, and patted cold water on his face before he looked at himself in the mirror. There were specks of dried blood on his hair. His left eye was swollen and bloodshot. His bony face was puffy, especially around the jaw and lips. There was a long scratch down the side of his nose, and another high on his right cheek. Not so bad. Looked worse that time I really fell off the stone fence. He grinned. Major and Hollis, for all their talk, they can't even rob a store or beat up a guy right. Just punks. Then he remembered that James was in jail, and the grin disappeared.

He walked into the front room, and sat down on the worn couch that opened into a double bed for Charlene and the twins. He turned on the television set.

A slim, pretty, white woman was standing in a shiny kitchen as big as Aunt Pearl's apartment, telling her tall, handsome husband how worried she was about Billy. He was spending all his free time in the garage and he wouldn't let anybody in except Gus, the dog. The husband puffed on his pipe and said he'd look into it, dear, and went outside, walking across a big lawn and under trees. He knocked on the garage door. Billy yelled, Who's there? Dad yelled back, The F.B.I., and there was tinny sounding laughter. Billy yelled, Just a minute, Dad, and there he was, about fourteen, scrambling around trying to hide the robot he was building. . . .

"Yeah, sure," said Alfred, snapping off the television.

He went back into his aunt's bedroom. The four voices on the street were getting louder ". . . num-ber one, on my top ten, you're . . .," but as soon as Alfred's head touched the pillow he was falling again into sleep.

The third time he awoke it was dusk. An occasional peal of drunken laughter drowned out the hoarse yells of tired children and the stoop chatter and the muted noise of a dozen transistors on different stations. He got up and went into the kitchen, enjoying the coolness of the cracked linoleum under his bare feet. The foldaway bed he usually slept in was tucked behind the refrigerator. He wondered if Aunt Pearl had slept in it, or stayed up all night. The sharp blue slacks he had worn were in a corner, next to Aunt Pearl's box of dusting rags. They were shredded. He put on a pair of clean cotton pants, and the blue tennis shirt with the little alligator on the pocket that Mrs. Elversen had given him for Christmas. He slipped on the black loafers that Jeff had outgrown. Cousin Jeff. Be hearing enough about him tomorrow.

He let himself out of the apartment quietly, so quietly that he surprised two drug addicts fumbling in the hall toilet. They looked up, startled, then saw it was only Alfred, and went back to their spoons and needles. For a moment he thought they were lucky, they'd be getting out of the world for a while, but then he remembered all the old-looking, sick junkies he saw on the streets, hunched-up, desperate for a fix.

"Major and Sonny been lookin' for you," said a little boy on the stoop. Alfred nodded, trying to look cool.

He went a few blocks out of his way so he could walk down an avenue where he knew he wouldn't meet Major. There were big cats there that even Major was afraid of, out to get him for something or other.

The cars were still cruising, guys with their Saturday night girls, guys looking for Saturday night girls. Live music floated out of an upstairs apartment, and there was a burst of laughter. Alfred jammed his hands into his pockets and walked faster. Half a dozen boys his age lounged on a corner, and one of them called to him. He just put his head down and walked on. Couples strolled by, arm in arm.

He looked up once, and saw Henry across the street, dragging his bad leg and smiling as if being crippled was the best thing in the world. Probably coming back from the gym, thought Alfred. Maybe tonight Mr. Donatelli let him wash the fighters' socks. Then he remembered that Henry had brought him home, and he dropped to his knees behind a parked car. When passersby stared at him, he pretended he was searching for a lost coin. He waited until Henry had turned the corner. He didn't feel like thanking anyone for anything tonight.

He crossed the street and started down a block he hardly ever walked on, a block of low apartment buildings, a store-front church, a delicatessen, a pawn shop, and on the corner, a bar. Above the bar, on a dusty plate-glass window, were the faded letters, DR. ARTHUR COREY, DENTIST. Above that, on a dustier window, in even more faded letters, DONATELLI'S GYM. A light was burning.

He stood on the corner for a long time, looking up at the dim light until his neck hurt and his eyes watered. A jukebox was blaring through the open door of the bar, but he barely heard it. DONATELLI'S GYM. The door leading up to the dentist's office and the gym was sagging off its hinges, half-open. Beyond it was darkness. DONATELLI'S GYM. Joe Louis had worked out there once. He remembered his father talking about how he had gone over to watch. Maybe Sugar Ray Robinson, too. They weren't no slaves, and they didn't have to bust into anybody's grocery store. They made it, they got to be somebody. He thought about going into the darkness, up to the dim light on the third floor. Maybe if James was around, we could both . . .

He turned to walk away and saw the familiar, muscular figure moving toward him with that rolling swagger. Major! Wildly, Alfred bolted across the street, side-stepping a taxicab by inches, ignoring the horns and curses of braking drivers. On the other side he glanced over his shoulder, and stopped. It wasn't Major after all. Slave. Always gonna be running, Alfred? And running alone?

He waited until the light turned green for him, and

he strode back across the street, up to the door. A quivering chill ran up his legs, and his teeth began to grind and a ball of ice formed in the pit of his stomach and he took a breath and plunged through the door, into the darkness, a choking, musty darkness that stank of stale wine and antiseptic and sweat and urine and liniment. He hit the first step, feeling it sag under him, but he kept going, up wooden steps worn so smooth his loafers slipped backwards, but the chilly legs were getting warmer now. Put one after another, Alfred, panting, huffing, low steps but hundreds of them, thousands of them in the darkness, the stairs so steep he sometimes fell to all fours, scrambling higher, past the sign, DR. COREY, past the sign, GYM-THIRD FLOOR, faster until his breath tangled in his ribs, higher until his throat was dry, faster, higher, until a door loomed before him. gym.

A faint light leaked through a crack, and he hurled himself up at it, paused, took another breath, and plunged into a large, murky room.

"Yeah?" A short, stocky man with crew-cut white hair looked up. His pale face was smooth and hard.

"I . . . I'm . . . I'm Alfred Brooks," he said, gasping. "I come . . . to be . . . a fighter."

The stocky man did not smile, or change his expression.

"Okay, Alfred Brooks," he said. "Take off your shirt."

Chapter 3

Donatelli circled slowly around him, his hand on his square chin, as if he were inspecting a slab of meat in a butcher store. He grabbed one of Alfred's hands, studying first the knuckles, then the palms.

"Big hands, you'll grow some more," he said. His voice was cold and rasping. He pointed at a battered white medical scale against a wall. "Get on."

Donatelli adjusted the vertical measure and fingered the sliding weights. "Five feet seven and three-quarter inches. One hundred twenty-four and a half pounds." There was no expression in his voice. He pointed at two wooden folding chairs facing each other. "Sit down."

Numbly, Alfred lowered himself to the edge of one chair, clutching his shirt in his hands. Donatelli sat down in the other, resting his heavy forearms on his neatly pressed gray slacks. His pale blue eyes flicked over Alfred's face and body. Alfred's eyes dropped down to the man's shoes, planted solidly on the wooden floor, black shoes curling with age but highly polished.

"Who sent you?"

"Nobody."

"Did you come by yourself?"

"Yes."

The pale blue eyes worked their way down to Alfred's hands, twisting and wringing the tennis shirt.

"Are you frightened?"

"Me? No, not—"

"A man must have some fear," said Donatelli,

"and learn to control it, to make it work for him. Do you understand?"

Alfred nodded.

"Have you ever boxed?"

"No."

"I can see you've been fighting in the street."

Donatelli stood up and marched across the room, his square, boxlike body erect. He pulled a string dangling from the ceiling, and a dozen naked bulbs flooded the large room with pools of yellow light. In the center of the room was a boxing ring, its white canvas floor stained and lumpy. Donatelli leaned against four black-taped ropes, and turned his bulldog face to Alfred.

"There's no place to hide in a boxing ring. You're all alone in there with another man who wants to hit you more times, and harder, than you hit him. There are rules, and there's a referee to make sure you follow them. It's not the street. You follow me?"

"Yes."

Donatelli nodded, his bushy white eyebrows arching over the cold eyes. "Sometimes kids come up here and they want to get in that ring right away and knock somebody's head off. No chance. You have to earn your way in there, you have to work hard for it. Most of the kids leave."

He straightened up and the ropes quivered back into place. One square, thick hand waved at a corner of the room. A gray, canvas bag, as large as a loaded army duffel bag, hung from the ceiling on a long chain.

"The heavy bag. Go on over and hit it. Not too hard."

Alfred walked across the room, the naked skin of his chest prickling. He punched the bag with his left fist. His knuckles burned and a sharp current of pain ran through his wrist, up his arm, exploding in his shoulder. The bag barely swayed.

"Over there," said Donatelli, pointing to another corner. A brown leather bag, not much larger than a paper lunch sack, hung from a swivel mounted on a round board screwed to the wall. "The peanut bag. Hit it a few times."

Alfred punched with his right, and the bag slapped against the round board. He missed with his left.

"The heavy bag is for power, to build up your arms and shoulders. The peanut bag is for speed and timing. Before you can go into the ring you have to be able to slam that heavy bag around all day and make that peanut bag sound like a machine gun."

"I could try," said Alfred.

"Thousands of kids can do it. Doesn't mean anything. The bag doesn't have any arms to hit you back with. You understand?"

"Yes."

"Let me tell you what it's like." He walked toward Alfred until they were standing face to face. His square head settled down into the crisp collar of his openthroated, short-sleeved white shirt. He had almost no neck.

"You get up at five-thirty in the morning, before the gas fumes foul the air, and you run in the park. That's to build up your legs and wind. You run smooth and easy, a little faster and a little longer each day. You run every day, rain or snow, unless you're too sick. Then you go home and eat breakfast. Juice, two boiled eggs, toast, and tea. You go to school?"

"I work."

"You don't eat too much lunch, it just makes you slow and tired. No fried foods, no beans, no cabbage, no pies and cakes, no soda. After work you come to the gym. Jump rope, stretching exercises, sit-ups, push-ups, deep-knee bends. You do them until you can't do any more, then you start all over again. You go home, have a good dinner. Meat, green vegetable, fresh salad, milk, fruit. You're asleep by nine o'clock."

Donatelli strolled beside the dusty plate-glass window. Neon signs blinked on and off in the street below, throwing pink, green, and blue mists against his smoothshaven cheeks. His thin lips barely moved as he talked. "You'll do it for a week, maybe two. You'll feel a little better physically, but all your friends, your family, will say you're a fool. You'll see other people smoking and drinking and staying out late, eating anything they want, and you'll start to think you're a fool, too. You'll say to yourself, 'All this sacrifice, and I'll probably never even get to be a good fighter.' And you'll be right, nine times out of ten."

His voice was lower as he moved away from the window and walked along a green wall, looking at the rusting clothes lockers and the faded posters advertising old prizefights.

"People will try to drag you down. Some will laugh, at you for wanting to be a fighter. And others will tell you you're so good you don't need to train, to go to bed early. How far did you go in school?"

"Eleventh grade."

"What happened?"

"I quit."

"Why?"

"Didn't seem like any reason to stay."

"What makes you think you won't quit here too?"

Alfred swallowed. He suddenly wished he hadn't come up the steps, that he was somewhere else, anywhere. He thought of the cave.

"Well?"

"I want to be somebody."

"Everybody is somebody."

"Somebody special. A champion."

Donatelli's thin lips tightened. "Everybody wants to be a champion. That's not enough. You have to start by wanting to be a contender, the man coming up, the man who knows there's a good chance he'll never get to the top, the man who's willing to sweat and bleed to get up as high as his legs and his brains and his heart will take him. That must sound corny to you."

"No."

"It's the climbing that makes the man. Getting to the top is an extra reward."

"I want to try."

Donatelli shrugged. "Boxing is a dying sport. People aren't much interested anymore. They want easy things like television, bowling, car rides. Get yourself a good job. Finish high school. Go at night if you have to."

"I'll try hard."

"Talk it over with your parents."

"I don't have any. I live with my aunt."

The pale blue eyes came around again. They seemed softer now. But the voice was still cold and flat. "It's not easy trying to become a contender. It's never any fun in the beginning. It's hard work, you'll want to quit at least once every day. If you quit before you really try, that's worse than never starting at all. And nothing's promised you, nothing's ever promised you."

He reached up and pulled the string. The room was murky again, except for the single light bulb. Donatelli spoke from the shadows.

"I'm always here, Alfred. I live here now. Whatever you decide, good luck to you." His footsteps echoed in the darkness as he walked away.

Alfred left. He moved carefully down the steps. They were still narrow and slippery, but no longer darkly threatening. He was halfway home before he realized that the twisted tennis shirt was still in his hand.

Chapter

"The white man's got his foot on your throat," roared the shave-skulled man on the stepladder. "You gonna lick his shoe?"

"Noooo, brother," chanted the street-corner crowd.

"He shoots you down in the street. You gonna keep turning the other cheek?"

"Hell-o, that's tellin' it."

Aunt Pearl sailed serenely past the nationalist rally, the three girls clustered around her like starched white tugboats escorting a blue cotton ocean liner. She looked neither right nor left, eyes focused straight ahead, her face glowing with the quiet joys of Sunday, her day. Alfred trailed a few steps behind, a strange new excitement bubbling in his stomach. He had hardly slept, the time in Donatelli's gym running through his mind all night, like a movie. But he felt more awake than he usually did on Sunday morning, and the streets seemed more alive than ever before.

The nationalist on the stepladder, his quick hands slashing through the air, was whipping his growing audience out of its morning listlessness.

"You gonna keep beggin' Whitey for crumbs off his table?"

"No."

"You gonna . . . Well, look at that." His forefinger stabbed out toward Alfred. "Ain't that sweet? On his way to pray to Whitey's God, learn to Tom and turn the other cheek . . ."

Alfred hurried on, away from the crowd's nervous laughter, past young men leaning against padlocked shop doors, tapping their shiny shoes and nodding their heads to silent music. He pushed through chattering families, past cool Ivy-League types and their light-skinned girl friends. He had almost caught up to his aunt's bobbing white hat when someone yelled, "Brooksy, hey Brooksy."

A stocky boy with horn-rimmed glasses came out of a crowd of young people lining up at the corner. He had a thick sheaf of leaflets under his arm. Alfred pretended he hadn't heard him, a big-shot politician he had never liked in high school.

"Come on with us, Brooksy, we're having a march," he said, grabbing Alfred's sleeve.

"Can't," said Alfred. "I'm going to church."

"We need you, man, come on," he said. Alfred shook his arm free. "Come on, we have to wake our people up, things are happening, man."

"Maybe later," said Alfred, starting to edge away as a slim girl joined the boy. "Not now."

"Now," she said firmly. "We want our rights now, and you can be part of this . . ."

"Save your breath, Lynn," said the boy. "Can't you see that Alfred Brooks is a happy little darky."

"Harold," snapped Lynn, "that's no way to get new . . ."

Alfred moved on, faster, angry at the sudden sting in his eyes, the sudden emptiness in his stomach. He brushed past the outstretched hand of a wino and caught up to his aunt and cousins. The serene look on Aunt Pearl's face calmed him at first, then made him angrier. Sometimes you'd think she was deaf, dumb, and blind, he thought.

The little store-front church was only half filled when they walked in, but Reverend Price was already behind the lectern, thumbing through his Bible. His wife, Sister Lucille, was in her tall wooden chair on one side of the pulpit. Aunt Pearl took her place up front with the choir, and the girls picked up their tambourines and sat in metal folding chairs behind her. Alfred took a chair toward the rear.

He tried to slide into his soft, dreamy Sunday morning trance, but it didn't come even when the hymns began and Aunt Pearl's pure, sweet voice rose above the others, filling the little room with a sound like golden honey. The other members of the congregation turned to watch her, as they always did, and most of them were smiling.

Reverend Price began to speak in his deep, heavy voice, the words booming out like beats on a muffled drum. Sister Lucille waved her arms, leading the congregation in the response.

". . . Amen, preacher, say it again," they chanted.

Somebody poked Alfred in the ribs. He turned. A man sitting near him pointed toward the back door. Alfred twisted around in his seat.

Major was standing in the doorway, his muscular hands clamped to his wide leather belt. Behind him Hollis was grinning, his big teeth hanging out over his lower lip. Alfred turned away quickly. The back of his neck began to itch and burn. He tried not to, but he had to turn around again. They were gone.

Services had never seemed so long, the metal chairs never seemed to have so many digging edges. He forced himself to listen to the sermon just to blot out the picture of Major and Hollis.

". . . The devil's agents wear new uniforms these trying days, but their poisons are the same. They say go out and hate the white man. They say go set yourself down in places where you are not wanted. They say . . ."

Alfred let the words wash over him. Devil's agents. What did they look like? Shaven skulls maybe, or big muscles. That pretty girl, Lynn, at the march. Was she a devil's agent? He'd have to ask James. James would roll his eyes that comical way he had and say, Alfred, my man, if she's a devil's agent I'm gonna go right down and apply for a . . . James. In jail now, maybe thinking I put him there. Pray they don't beat him too bad.

The morning services finally ended. The children turned their tambourines upside down and took the collection. Aunt Pearl was the last one out, telling the Reverend how much she enjoyed his sermon, how sad she was at having to miss his afternoon teachings. She probably is, thought Alfred.

The subway ride out to Jamaica took more than an hour. Aunt Pearl kept her eyes closed, as if she were still in prayer, except when Charlene, Sandra, and Paula got restless and started giggling among themselves. Then she opened her eyes and scowled them into silence. It was hot in the subway car. Big black fans turned slowly on the ceiling, moving the hot air around and spinning off bits of soot. The splintery wicker of the subway seat pressed through his damp pants.

A pretty girl his age came aboard wearing a fresh-looking pink dress, and sat opposite him. Her skin was smooth and cocoa-colored, and she stared right back at him through oversized sunglasses. Alfred looked away first, wishing something would happen, the train would get stuck between stations, the girl would fall down and need help, anything so he could walk over, suave and sophisticated, "I'm Alfred Brooks, may I be of service?"—just like in the movies.

But the train reached Jamaica without any trouble, and their bus was waiting at the corner. They rode past grimy little factories and projects and, after a while, along clean, grassy streets lined with neat little houses. Aunt Pearl was always so proud that one of her sisters married a man with a good job who bought her a house in Queens. Just before they got off the bus, Aunt Pearl leaned over and whispered, "Lord help me, Alfred, but I told Dorothy and Wilson on the phone how you fell off that stone fence. Be no need to say nothing else."

Aunt Dorothy, tall and bony, was waiting at the front door with her own small daughter, Diane. She hugged the three little girls and Aunt Pearl, then hooked her arm into Alfred's, kissed him on the cheek, and pulled him inside. Uncle Wilson, tall and bony, too, loped across the front room and dropped a big hand on Alfred's shoulder. "You're getting taller, boy, you're gonna be big as Jeff one of these days."

They sat down to eat right away—cold chicken, thick slices of ham and cheese, potato salad, macaroni salad, bread, plenty of lemonade, a seven-layer cake. Uncle Wilson, Alfred, and the four girls dug in, but Pearl and Dorothy, acting as if they didn't talk on the phone at least twice a week, chattered away, picking daintily at their food. Afterwards the girls ran upstairs to Diane's room, and Aunt Dorothy and Aunt Pearl cleared the table and went into the kitchen. Alfred followed his uncle out to the back porch and watched him carefully fill his pipe and light it. The afternoon sun made shadows on his uncle's bony face, deepening the hollows under his cheekbones. Wilson rocked in his chair and pointed his pipe stem at Alfred.

"Still at the grocery store?"

"Yes."

"Like it there?"

"It's all right."

"Opportunity for advancement?"

Alfred shrugged.

"You got to be thinking ahead, Alfred. World is changing, opening up for colored people." He sucked on his pipe, staring out at a row of purple flowers.

"Yes, sir, Alfred, world is changing. Me, I never was past the county line until the war came. Now your cousin Jeff's been all over the country. Talkin' about joining the Peace Corps after college, go to Africa. Got a letter from him the other day, says he's going to be ready when the opportunities come." Uncle Wilson smiled into the cloud of smoke rising from his pipe, and he crossed his bony legs.

"Been thinking about your future, Alfred?"

"Some."

"The trades is opening up. Electricians, carpenters, bricklayers make good money these days. They'll be more places for colored people soon. But you have to be ready, have to have your education. Have to be qualified. You think about the trades at all?"

"Sometimes."

"Jeff says he might go into law, maybe teaching. He's going South this summer, work in those voter registration schools. Says once colored people are all voting the—what's he call it?—yeah, the white power structure going to find more jobs for them, more opportunities for advancement. World is changing."

They lapsed into silence, Wilson comparing his pipe clouds, Alfred slouching in the porch chair. He could hear the girls giggling upstairs, and the chatter of the women in the kitchen. He tried to remember Jeff. He must be nineteen or twenty now, very tall, taller than his father and bigger across the chest and shoulders. He had only seen Jeff a few times in the last three years since he went away to college. But he always heard about Jeff, winning all the prizes at high school graduation, a scholarship to college. And he had to look at all the pictures—Jeff in a tuxedo at his freshman prom, Jeff being sworn in as president of his sophomore class, Jeff shaking hands with somebody important. He sank deeper into the chair, feeling all the good food lying heavily on his stomach.

Wilson rocked and smoked, and after a while they talked about the Yankees and how the Mets' pitching was perking up. Alfred felt better then. It was peaceful out here. Uncle Wilson and his pipe seemed so strong and wise. For one wild moment he wanted to tell him about Mr. Donatelli, but he swallowed it back and the moment passed. The light began to fade, and Dorothy called them in for more cake and lemonade, and then it was time to calm down the girls, who were cranky, say good-bye, and start back to Harlem.

"You think about the trades, Alfred," said Uncle Wilson, and then the bus came.

Aunt Pearl and the girls dozed on the subway, but Alfred wasn't tired. He watched a huge black man, drunk and bleeding from a cut on his head, sprawl out in the middle of the car and go to sleep. Twice, when the train lurched, he sat up, looking around fiercely. Alfred tensed, wondering how he could stop the man if he went crazy and attacked Aunt Pearl or the girls. But each time, the man lay down, smiling sweetly, and went back to sleep.

The streets seemed dirtier when they got out, and the apartment seemed smaller. It always happened after visiting in Queens. Alfred helped Aunt Pearl open the couch and put the girls to sleep. Then they sat down in the kitchen and drank some milk.

"What's troubling you, Alfred?"

"What made you ask that?"

"You been so quiet. You thinking about James?"

"Some."

"You want to talk about it?"

"Not right now."

"When you do, honey, you know you can always talk to me." She kissed him on the forehead and went into her bedroom.

Alfred unfolded his bed, and sat down on the edge, staring at the green-painted plaster beginning to crack over the kitchen sink. A roach scurried over the cabinet, paused, then scurried back into the wall. There was a scuffling noise out in the hall. The addicts.

Tomorrow was Monday, blue Monday, dirty Monday. The store would be filthy, there would be dozens of cartons and cans to stack. Opportunity for advancement? Sure, they might even let me deliver on the bicycle. He saw Major shuffle along the clubroom floor. Uncle Alfred. The Epsteins would be asking about the attempted robbery. About James. He would scratch his head and play dumb, like you always do when the white man asks those questions you better not answer. He's got his foot on your throat, you gonna lick his shoe? Come march with us, Alfred. Maybe later. Happy little darky. World is opening up for colored people. Devil's got new uniforms. We'll get you. Everybody wants to be a champion, Alfred. Slave. Nothing's promised you. Slave. Opportunity for advancement? You have to start by wanting to be a contender.

He stood up quietly, and tiptoed into his aunt's room. She was snoring. He took the alarm clock from her bureau and put it on the kitchen cabinet. He stared at it for a long time before he set it for five-thirty. Then he snapped off the light. He kept waking up through the night, listening for the tick, staring at the glowing hands. Had he set it right, was it wound up enough, was the alarm button pulled out?

The last time he looked at the clock it was quarter to four, and the faintest tinge of pink was brushing the window.

Chapter 5

The grass was spongy with dew and the air was cool and sweet, filling his lungs until they pressed against his ribs and a stitch ran up and down his side. Then he was crunching over gravel. The sky was blood-red. It was going to be another warm day but not yet. He couldn't help smiling, he'd sing if he had the breath. He was all alone in the park. The birds were chattering in the overhanging trees, sitting on their stoops telling all the bird gossip. Smooth and easy, Alfred, build up the wind and the legs, smooth and easy, pick up those feet. The breeze streamed past his cheeks, cooling, and the muscles of his legs stretched and got warm and his elbows swung along his sides and the silly smile grew wider and he thought he'd burst from the joy of . . .

"Hold it right there."

Two policemen stepped out from behind a bush, and the birds stopped their chatter.

"Where you going this time of morning?"

"I'm running."

"I can see that," said the smaller cop. "Where you running to?"

"Just running, officer. I'm in training."

"For what?" asked the bigger cop.

"Boxing," said Alfred.

The two policemen looked at each other, and the little one winked. "Oh, yeah, I know you. Fighting for the heavyweight championship of the world next week, right?"

Alfred shook his head. His mouth suddenly felt dry

and gritty and his tongue thick. "Just starting."

"Who's your manager?"

"Mr. Donatelli."

The big cop nodded. "I've heard of him. Had three champions, two at the same time, I think. What's your name, boy?"

"Alfred Brooks."

"Okay, Al, you keep training. We'll look for your picture in the papers." They laughed and disappeared back into the bushes.

The spring was out of his step, and suddenly the stitch seemed unbearable, and he could hear cars moving through the park. Gas fumes. That's enough for today, he thought, knowing it wasn't, and he slowed down again and started trudging back to the apartment. The good feeling was gone. His sneakers felt heavy, as if they were filled with water.

Aunt Pearl was bustling around the kitchen, getting the girls ready for school when he came in.

"Alfred. Where you been? Are you just getting in now? You been out all night?"

"Took a walk."

"A walk?"

Sandra saved him, screaming that Paula had hidden her hair ribbons. Aunt Pearl got busy quieting them down, feeding them breakfast, helping Charlene make the lunch sandwiches. When the girls finally left for school, Aunt Pearl turned back to Alfred, her eyebrows raised.

"Now. Where you been?"

"Just went out. Couldn't sleep."

"Where you been you need the alarm clock?"

"Took a walk."

"You said that already, Alfred. You look at me now. Are you in trouble?"

"No."

Her voice dropped to a whisper. "Somebody after you for something?"

"No."

"I ain't gonna press you, Alfred, you do a man's work and I ain't gonna treat you like a boy. But I know something's wrong. We eat all right, don't we?"

"Yes."

"We ain't on welfare, the rent's paid up, we got nice Sunday clothes. We're doin' all right. Did your Uncle Wilson get you all upset?"

"Uncle Wilson?"

"I heard him braggin' about Jeff. You do all right too. You got a job, you . . ."

"Big job."

"Alfred! You be glad you're workin'. Streets are full of men hangin' around, waitin' for trouble."

"I'm gonna be somebody," he said, feeling his throat tighten up again.

She surrounded him with her soft arms. "You somebody right now, Alfred. A good, God-fearing boy, minds his aunt, helps . . ."

"Somebody special," he said, pulling away.

She dropped her arms and took a step back, peering up into his face. "How you mean, Alfred?"

He shrugged. "Some way."

"Alfred," she whispered, "you wasn't really fixin' to go with James that night . . . Alfred!"

She was still calling his name as he ran out the door.

Lou Epstein, the oldest, shortest, and baldest of the three Epstein brothers, barely looked up from the cash register when Alfred entered the store.

"I want to talk to you," he said.

He signaled to Jake, the middle brother, to take over the cash register. He led Alfred back to the storeroom. Ben, the youngest brother, was licking a black crayon and marking prices on soap-flake boxes when they walked in. Lou jerked his bald head, and Ben left the room.

"Some boys tried to break into the store Friday night. You hear about it?"

"No."

"That friend of yours, James Mosely. The police caught him. Put him in jail over the weekend."

There was a long silence, and Alfred studied the green vegetable stains on Lou's apron. "What are they going to do with him?"

"They'll let him go on probation. First offense, and nothing was stolen. You didn't even hear about it?"

"I heard something."

"You heard something." Lou rubbed his pale scalp. "You heard maybe who the other boys were?"

Alfred shook his head and lowered his eyes to Lou's shoes. They were worn and cracked, with holes for Lou's bunions.

"You're a good boy, Alfred, we all think you're a good boy. I told the police not to bother you. But sometimes it's hard to . . . well, we trust you, but for your own sake there's no point tempting fate. You understand."

Alfred shook his head again, and Lou shrugged his thin shoulders. "We'll see, we'll see. Okay. After you get done sweeping up, help Ben with the new crates." He went back to the cash register.

They said very little through the morning. Jake kept shooting glances at Alfred out of the corner of his eye. Even Ben was quiet, Ben who always asked Alfred how he had spent his weekend, and then winked knowingly when Alfred said he had seen some movies, watched television, and hung around. There was tension in the store, as thick and heavy as the air before a rainstorm. Aunt Pearl sensed it too, when she came in on her way to work. She didn't say anything about Alfred's leaving without breakfast or forgetting his lunch. She just put the paper bag on the counter and walked out, frowning.

He ate in the back of the store, alone, chewing sandwiches that tasted like cardboard in his dry mouth. The Epsteins always let him take a soda or milk and a piece of fruit. But today he felt too uncomfortable to pick out the rest of his lunch.

The afternoon was hot. Flies buzzed in through the door, landing on the open watermelons and the sweet corn, climbing up the sweating pickle barrel. Two heavy-set white men, perspiring through their summer suits, came in and whispered with Jake and Lou. They looked like detectives to Alfred. One of them wrote something in a black leather notebook, nodded, and snapped it shut.

"We'll stay in touch, Lou. Bet you're glad now you took our advice on that new alarm."

There was plenty of work to do, and he could pretend to concentrate hard on peeling the rotten leaves off the cabbages or sponging the spilt milk from the refrigerator floor. He was arranging the fruit in the front window, half-watching Lonny, the sixty-year-old delivery boy, park his bicycle, when he first saw James. The round face, swollen and grim, was framed between hand-printed window signs advertising the week's special sales.

"Hey," Alfred called, starting toward the door. He stopped at the cold, hard look in James' eyes. James turned and swaggered away. Like Major.

At quarter to three, Lou Epstein banged open the lower cash drawer and counted the big bills into a brown envelope. Alfred went to the back to wash his hands while Lou filled out the deposit slip. When he came out, Jake was stuffing the envelope into a pocket. Sure, thought Alfred, now I understand about no point tempting fate. They don't even trust me to go to the bank anymore.

There was little to do in the late afternoon. Alfred swept and reswept the dark wooden floor just to keep moving, his head down, avoiding the Epsteins' sad, distrustful looks. He kept remembering how good he had felt in the park, jogging over the gravel, the wind in his face, his muscles heating up. Hold it right there, said the cop. He kept seeing James' face on the wooden floor, cold eyes in a swollen face.

He swept his way into the back room, jamming the straw broom into nooks and crannies he had already swept clean. The tiny wires of the new burglar alarm snaked along the molding of the back door, and for an instant he thought of sweeping them loose, one good, hard swipe should do it. Come back at night, get in the back . . . Wait until next Friday when there would be a lot of money in the register. . . . Come back with James, then he'd know I didn't purposely let him walk into a trap. He swept his way out among the shelves. Can't do it. Maybe never be able to do anything but sweep up this crummy store.

Nothing's promised you, that's what Mr. Donatelli said. Why'd I have to go up there, listen to all that foolishness, get excited about it like a little kid? Glad nobody but those cops saw me running this morning, that was foolishness, too. Hold it right there, said the cop. Slave, said Major. Good boy, said Lou.

Alfred felt in his pocket. Enough for a nice dark movie, he thought, sit and watch it forever.

"Hey, Alfred."

He looked up, startled. "Henry."

"What time you comin' by?"

"Where?" He stared at the ever-grinning face

peering in through the door.

"The gym."

"Gym?"

"Yeah. Mr. Donatelli said you was up Saturday night. He asked me about you."

"What you tell him—"

"Gotta run. See you later."

"Henry." But he was gone.

Chapter 6

He bounced up the steps two at a time, friendly old steps, trying not to grin like a fool because Mr. Donatelli would give him that blue-eyed once-over and you better look tough and all-business on day number one. He hit the door and stepped in, and his jaw dropped. The gym looked like Reverend Price's Hell.

Half-naked bodies were jumping and twisting and jerking around, bells rang, the peanut bag went *rackety-rackety-rackety*, ropes swish-slapped against the squeaking floorboards, someone screamed, "TIME," gasping voices, "Uh . . . uh . . . uh-uh," and an enormous black belly rushed past, spraying sweat like a lawn sprinkler. Alfred shrank back against the door.

Slowly he picked out objects he had seen before. The heavy bag was swinging wildly on its chain as the boy with the enormous belly battered it with fists as big as cantaloupes. The peanut bag was rattling against the round board as a skinny white boy with hunched shoulders beat it into a brown blur. Near the medical scale, two Puerto Ricans were jabbing at their reflections in full-length mirrors. They were quick as cats. Other boys were jumping rope, jerking up and down like mechanical jacks-in-the-box, or straining on leather floor mats until their neck cords popped, or slamming medicine balls into each other's stomachs. In the ring, their heads encased by black leather guards, two fighters danced around each other, ducking, bobbing, bouncing on and off the quivering ropes. A stick-thin old black man with white hair was yelling at them, "Faster, faster, pick it up."

The room began to shrink, and the noise pounded against Alfred's head. He looked around for Mr. Donatelli or Henry, but neither was in the room. He saw an old sign on the wall.

Amateurs—$2 weekly
Professionals—$5 weekly
PAYABLE IN ADVANCE

He felt for his wallet. There would be at least two dollars in it, but there was no one around to take his money or tell him what to do. No one was even looking at him. Leave now, he thought, come back some other time, when it's less crowded, when Henry's around. But something told him if he left now he would never come back. He waited, watching the thin man unstrap the fighters' headguards and shake a black pencil of a finger in their faces. He watched the enormous belly move lightly across the room toward the peanut bag, and take over when the skinny white boy dropped his arms and shuffled away. The Puerto Ricans climbed into the ring, and the rope jumpers began shadowboxing. Everyone seemed to know what to do. Some other time, he thought, edging backwards out the door, turning so quickly that he never saw the chubby little man until his elbow banged into a soft chest.

"Uhh."

"Oh, I'm sorry, I—"

The little man held up a small hand. "That's an illegal punch."

"I didn't mean to—"

"If the referee saw that you'd lose the round.

Automatically." He was smiling, his reddish cheeks puffed out like a squirrel's.

"I wasn't looking."

"No harm done. Your first day?"

"Yes, Mr. Donatelli said—"

"He's not here today, one of his boys has a fight at the Garden tonight."

"I'll come back some other—"

"Today's better than tomorrow. What's your name?"

"Alfred Brooks."

"I'm Dr. Corey."

"The dentist downstairs?"

"Aha. Alertness." The little red face moved closer, and tiny gray eyes blinked behind thick spectacles. "For that I will offer you a pearl of wisdom. Are you ready?"

"Yes," said Alfred, feeling his jaw relax.

"The stomach is more important than the chin. Hit the chin and you may break your hand. Kill the belly and the head will die. Do you read me?"

"I don't think so."

The dentist shrugged. "I am too far ahead of my time. Start with sit-ups, Alfred. Make your stomach like a rock." Huffing slightly, he walked over to the ring. The thin man smiled and patted him on the shoulder.

Alfred walked over to the floor mats. Two boys, in gym clothes and boxing shoes, were balancing themselves on their shoulders, kicking their legs up in the air. One was the skinny white boy, the other was well-built with light skin and reddish hair. Alfred waited until they finished the exercise before he lowered himself to a corner of a mat.

"You gon' work out in street clothes?" asked the redhead.

"All I got," said Alfred.

"Let any trash in nowadays," he grumbled, rolling over and starting push-ups.

Alfred stretched out on his back, putting his hands under his head and pointing his toes. He jerked up fast, went back down, and jerked up fast again. In high school gym class he had always been good at sit-ups.

"What you call them?" asked the redhead.

"Sit-ups."

"Haw. You hear that, Denny? He calls them sit-ups." The redhead laughed and poked the white boy.

"So show him how to do it, Red," said Denny, looking annoyed.

"Don't waste my time with trash," said Red, getting up and walking away.

"Let me show you," said Denny, rolling over on his back. The scrawny body came up very slowly, quivering with the strain, folding over until the face and the knees were almost touching. Then Denny went back down again, even more slowly.

"Thanks," said Alfred.

"You bet," said Denny.

Alfred tried it, coming up slowly, inch by inch, fighting to keep his legs straight and his heels on the mat as his shoulders began to quiver and the muscles in his stomach tightened painfully. Up and then over, toward his knees, feeling the long muscles in his thighs pull and his back muscles tear, until the blood flooded his head and he couldn't go any further. Then slowly back down again, his body shuddering, till slowly, gently, he lowered the back of his head to the mat. He took a deep breath, and the pain faded away.

"That right?" he asked, but Denny was already on the other side of the room, skipping rope.

The second sit-up was harder than the first, and

the third was harder still. But by the fourth his muscles began to get warm, like a car engine heating up on a cold morning, and they stopped struggling against each other. He did twenty sit-ups before he fell back exhausted. Not bad, he thought, been such a long time. He sat up and looked around. Dr. Corey and the thin man were talking at ringside. Boxers were grunting away all over the gym. No Henry.

He turned over and started on push-ups, slowly, concentrating on keeping his body straight. After thirty-four push-ups his arms felt rubbery.

"Hey, Alfred, been here long?" Henry dragged up, a box under his arm. "Had to go downtown, pick up something for Bud."

"Who's Bud?"

"Bud Martin, Mr. Donatelli's assistant," said Henry, pointing at the thin man. "See you later."

"Hey, Henry."

"Yeah?" Henry turned impatiently.

Alfred tried to think of something to say, anything to keep Henry from leaving. His eyes fell on the sign. "Do I have to pay my two dollars now?"

"No. When you can spare it easy. If you can't pay, Mr. Donatelli won't throw you out."

"Henry," called Bud Martin.

"Right there."

Alfred did a few more sit-ups, but the sweat running under his street clothes began to itch. Some of the boxers were weighing themselves, and joking, and drifting off into the shower room behind the rusty lockers. The gym was quieting down. The peanut bag was silent. Dr. Corey passed him on the way out, but didn't look down. Henry was over in a corner, helping Bud Martin pack a black satchel. Alfred was alone again. He felt another urge to leave, but he forced himself to stroll over toward Henry and

Bud, his hands in his pockets, casual, so no one could tell he felt out of place.

Up close, Alfred could see Bud Martin's ribs pushing through his tattered T-shirt. But the bony hands were sure and quick as the old man stuffed small jars and rolls of tape into the valise.

"Hey, Bud," shouted Red, shouldering past Alfred.

Bud didn't look up. "Need some more cotton tips, Henry."

"Sure." Henry disappeared back into the dressing room.

"I'm talkin' to you, Bud," said Red.

"Talk," snapped Bud.

"I need my hands taped."

"You learn to do it yourself."

"Willie Streeter don't have to do it himself."

Bud looked up, his black eyes hard in the skull face. Muscles all over his face twitched underneath the drumtight skin when he talked. "But Willie knows how, and there's a difference right there."

Red mumbled something and walked away, again brushing Alfred.

"Some people," said Bud, "think this is a nursery school. Henry?"

"I got the cotton tips," said Henry, putting a cellophane package in Bud's hand.

"Better bring me another jar of Vaseline."

"Right."

"Always use a lot of Vaseline on Willie's face," said Bud, talking mostly into the black satchel. "He's got dry skin that cuts so easy. Sometimes even the grease don't help."

"What happens if he gets cut?" asked Alfred.

Bud reached into the satchel and pulled out a small jar of yellowish paste. "Stops the bleeding, keeps the cut clean."

"What is it?"

"Clarence Martin's Magical Potion. Patent Pending."

"What's in it?"

Bud winked. "I got doctors call me from California ask what's in it."

"Do you tell them?"

"You crazy, boy? Only Donatelli and me knows what's in it, and even he don't know exactly how much of each special ingredient I use."

"Like a trade secret?"

"Exactly." Bud grinned, showing pink, toothless gums. "I invented it forty-one years ago. Had this lightweight, skin so thin would start bleeding if his mother kissed him. Lightning Lou Epp, real good little—"

"I need a headguard," said Red.

"I'll get it," said Henry, limping up with the Vaseline jar.

"Stay where you're at, Henry," said Bud. "Now, what you need a headguard for?"

"Gon' spar."

"You know the rules, boy. No sparring unless the boss or me is watching. He's not here, and I ain't got time."

"Don't be an old woman," said Red.

"If you don't know the rules maybe you don't belong here."

"I pay my dues. I belong here more than a lot of people."

"Rules the same for everybody," said Bud.

"Just get me a headguard."

The room fell quiet. Whoever had started punching the peanut bag stopped, letting it squeak into silence on the swivel. The Puerto Rican boys,

Denny, the enormous belly, the others, moved into a circle around Alfred, Henry, Red, and Bud.

"Ever since you come," said Bud softly, looking into the satchel, "you been a smart meat. Be sweet, boy. Joe Louis been up here and he had a good word for everybody. Sugar Ray and Cassius Clay been up and treated everyone fine."

"Skip the lip," said Red. "Your job's to get me a headguard when I want it."

"My job's to help Mr. Donatelli train you how to fight. But you got to get to be a man on your own."

"You saying I ain't a man, you old crow?" Red's hands came up. Alfred saw they were taped.

"You wanna fight somebody you fight me," said the enormous belly, pushing Alfred out of his way. "I say you ain't no man, neither."

"Mind your business, Jelly Belly," said Bud. Carefully, he took the Vaseline jar from Henry's outstretched hand and placed it in the satchel. He snapped the satchel shut, and looked up.

"Now. What's your problem, boy?"

Red leaned forward, his skin flushing with sudden blood. Bud's gaunt face seemed to get blacker.

"If you had any teeth I'd knock 'em out," said Red.

"Go make believe I got teeth."

Red's right hand balled into a fist, and the arm shot out like a jackhammer, straight at Bud's mouth. The old man never blinked, lazily waving his left arm, knocking Red's hand aside. One skinny black hand whipped out and cracked against Red's jaw.

Red backed up, tears springing to his eyes. Alfred suddenly felt sorry for him. Red ran to his locker, pulled out his clothes, and bolted out of the gym.

Bud looked around. "Don't nobody tell the boss about this. Everybody gets a second chance around here. Now go on with what you were doin'. Show's over."

The others drifted away, and Bud fingered the lock on the satchel. "Nobody ever said it was easy. Got to come up here, day after day, got to put out, and some days nobody even looks at you 'cept to say you're doin' something wrong."

He locked the satchel. "That's part of it. You hungry enough, you keep at it." He looked right at Alfred. "You Alfred Brooks?"

"Yes."

"Figured. Tonight you gonna see a real fight, no slappin'."

"Me?"

"Yeah. Henry's got your ticket. The boss said if you ever came back you might as well see what you came back for."

Chapter 7

Hundreds of people milled under the marquee of Madison Square Garden as Alfred and Henry came up from the subway. Seedy men with mashed-in faces waved their cigars at tall, well-dressed businessmen carrying attaché cases. Big, rough teen-agers jostled through the crowd, their sleeves rolled high enough to show off blue and red tattoos. Young white girls with piles of golden hair hung on the arms of flashily dressed men. Alfred's nose tingled. The smells of perfume and after-shave lotion and mustard and beer were mixed together. The sharpest of all were the big-time Harlem gamblers in white dinner jackets, elegantly stepping with glittering women who looked as though they posed for the advertisements in *Ebony* magazine.

"C'mon, Alfred," said Henry, pulling his sleeve.

At the ticket window, a fat-faced white man scowled down at them, and Alfred was sure he would tell them to get lost. But Henry said, "Mr. Donatelli left two for Henry Johnson," and a little white envelope slid out between the bars.

The man who took their tickets at the door scowled, and Alfred was sure he wouldn't let them in, but he tore the tickets without a word and returned the stubs. Then he turned to scowl at a white couple right behind them. The usher scowled, and the man selling programs scowled, and the man behind the frankfurter stand scowled, and the guard who checked their tickets at the black curtain scowled, and then they were inside the Garden.

Alfred caught his breath. It was huge. It was almost a circle, and the seats rose right up the walls toward a ceiling of cables and beams. In the center of the floor, gleaming white under hundreds of spotlights, was the ring. The ropes were wrapped in red velvet.

"Keep movin'." Someone stepped on the back of his shoe, and Alfred stumbled on. Three more scowling men, in blue uniforms, pointed them on until they reached their seats—attached wooden chairs on the arena floor ten rows away from the ring.

A dignified little man in a bright blue tuxedo climbed through the ropes and pulled down a microphone from the tangle of wires and blazing lights over the ring. He asked them all to please rise for the national anthem. The music swelled out of an organ and boomed through the half-empty arena, sending little shivers up Alfred's spine.

"Hey, brothers, how's it goin'?" Jelly Belly plopped into a seat next to Henry, his great stomach bouncing under a pink sport shirt. He peered over at Alfred. "You the one nearly got caught in the middle of that thing today? Yeah, didn't recognize you in the Sunday suit."

Self-consciously, Alfred began to loosen his tie, but Jelly Belly tapped his hand. "Don't, brother, we need a little class around here."

"Did you see Willie?" asked Henry.

"Just came from him," said Jelly Belly.

"How is he?"

"He's Willie, y'know what I mean? Mr. Donatelli's in there, telling him just how to fight Becker and Willie is nodding his head and everybody knows, sure as hunger, Willie's gonna go in there and do it *his* way."

"I read in the paper coming down here," said Alfred, "that Willie Streeter could be the next champion."

"Mr. Donatelli's counting on it," said Henry.

Jelly Belly bounced up. "Chow time. Anybody want a hot dog?" He waved at one of the hot dog vendors.

"Hey, Jelly," said Henry, "you know Mr. Donatelli said you gotta cut down on all that—"

"You lightweights gotta worry about the pounds," said Jelly, winking at Alfred, "but us heavies need to keep up our strength."

The preliminary bouts were a blur of bodies and punches for Alfred, but he jumped up every time Henry and Jelly did. He nodded when Jelly poked him and said, "Some hook Chico's got, huh?", and he tried to look knowing when Henry yelled, "Y'ever see footwork like that, Alfred?"

He tried to follow the action, but he kept thinking about the day he and James found the boxing and wrestling magazine on the street. They flipped right past the boxing section to the wrestling pictures. James decided they should become professional wrestlers, and he made up their names. Mosely of the Jungle and Bad Brooks. When they got back to Alfred's stoop, James started jumping up and down, pounding on his chunky chest and howling so loud people leaned out of their windows to watch. Alfred fell off the stoop laughing, and James ran down and put a foot on his stomach. An old lady stared at them, and James growled, "That's how Mosely of the Jungle triumphs. They all die laughing." Alfred tried to push the thought away and concentrate on the fights.

"Here we go," said Henry.

Mr. Donatelli, solid and square, moved down the

aisle, clearing a path for Willie Streeter, a tall, handsome Negro who waved to the crowd. He wore a white robe with his name on the back. Bud Martin and Dr. Corey were right behind him. The crowd started cheering and clapping even before Willie slipped gracefully through the ropes into the ring, and sat down on a three-legged stool. He sat there quietly, as Donatelli whispered in his ear and Dr. Corey and Bud knelt to massage his arms and legs. The three older men were wearing long-sleeved white sweaters with willie streeeter written across the back in red letters.

The ring announcer pulled the microphone down again. "Ladeeez . . . and gentlemen. A ten-round bout. In this corner, wearing black trunks and weighing one hundred seventy-four pounds, from Houston, Texas . . . Junius Becker."

There was some polite applause and a few boos. Half a dozen people sitting together near ringside cheered for Becker.

"And in this corner, in white trunks"—the crowd began to cheer loudly and steadily—"weighing one hundred seventy-four and one-half pounds, from New York City . . . Willie Streeter."

The cheering and the applause grew as Willie stood up. He smiled and waved a red glove at the crowd. So cool, thought Alfred. So confident. He settled back to watch Willie beat up poor old Junius.

The first few rounds were slow. Willie and Junius were circling, throwing out punches that were easy to duck or knock away. Henry was squirming in his seat, "Stick him, Willie, keep him off balance."

Jelly, his voice becoming shrill, shouted, "Move in on 'im, Willie, please, Willie."

Between the rounds, Willie nodded as Donatelli whispered in his ear. Alfred tried to imagine himself up there, taking a long drink of water from the taped-up bottle in Bud's hand, spitting it out in one long stream into a bucket, opening his mouth so Dr. Corey could jam in the white mouthpiece.

The bell rang, and both fighters rushed together, Willie's left arm pumping out like a machine, slamming into Becker's face, rocking him backward against the red velvet ropes.

"Keep on 'im, Willie, don't let him rest," shrieked Jelly.

Henry shouted, "Stick, stick . . . Look at him, Alfred, he's . . ."

Whatever Henry said next was swallowed in the crowd's roar as the two fighters smashed into each other, banging heads and stumbling backwards. Becker fell to one knee, his gloves on the canvas floor.

The referee began counting, "One . . . two . . . three . . ." Becker shook his head, as if to clear it. ". . . four . . . five . . . six . . ." Then he climbed to his feet. ". . . seven . . . eight." The referee wiped Becker's gloves on his gray shirt and stepped aside, signaling the two men to continue boxing.

Suddenly the crowd went, "Ooooohhhhh," and Jelly leaned toward Alfred. "He's hurt."

Willie was bleeding. It looked like a deep cut to Alfred, right on the outside corner of Willie's left eye.

"Willie's in trouble," said Jelly.

Alfred saw it immediately. Becker was aiming his punches at the bleeding eye, and all the fight seemed to be draining out of Willie. He wasn't attacking anymore, he was just dancing backwards, his gloves up in front of his face. Becker rushed in, punching away at the unprotected belly. All Willie's coolness and confidence seemed to be gone.

At the end of the round, Donatelli, Bud, and Dr. Corey swarmed over Willie. Bud moved in with a gob of yellowish paste on the tip of his finger, but the manager waved it away. He peered at the cut eye and called over the referee. Suddenly, the crowd was booing and Junius Becker was waving his arms and Willie Streeter was trying to struggle away from Bud and the dentist.

"What happened?" asked Alfred.

"Technical knockout, TKO," said Henry. "Mr. Donatelli had the fight stopped."

The crowd continued to boo as Donatelli and Bud each grabbed one of Willie's arms and dragged him down the ring steps and up the aisle.

Jelly jumped up. "Come on," he said.

It took them fifteen minutes to work their way through the crowd, even with Jelly's belly leading the way. On all sides the booing rose, and a man cupped flabby hands around his mouth and yelled, "Ya sissy, I cut myself worse shaving every morning."

They finally entered a long, dim tunnel. A big guard stood cross-armed in front of a closed door.

"Sorry, fellas, you can't come . . . Oh, Jelly, how are ya?" He unlocked the door and waved them into a large room, bare except for some benches and old lockers. Willie was sitting on an upholstered table, clenching and unclenching his taped hands as a doctor worked on his eye. Donatelli was whispering to him, and Bud and Dr. Corey were shaking their heads. Two men with State Athletic Commission badges on their jackets were staring up at the ceiling. The only other person in the room, a husky young man with a broken nose, came over to Jelly, his hand outstretched.

"My man Spoon," said Jelly, grabbing the hand. "What's the mood?"

"Not good," whispered Spoon, loosening his tie from his button-down collar.

"How's Willie taking it?"

"We'll see in a minute."

The doctor put a strip of white adhesive tape over Willie's cut, and left. Willie touched it, tapped it, blinked his eye, and whirled on Donatelli. "I woulda won and you know it, I woulda won that fight, I woulda . . ."

The manager's face reddened, and it seemed to Alfred that he swallowed down something he was about to say.

"Look, Willie, do you want to go through life with one eye, for one lousy fight?"

"Nothing wrong with my eye," yelled Willie, as Donatelli, his mouth a slit, turned away. "You can't even look at me after what you did, throwin' in the towel like that."

"Talk about it tomorrow," said Donatelli.

"Right now," yelled Willie, jumping off the table. His eyes swept his audience, all looking at their shoes. "If you're scared of a little blood, I can get a manager who isn't."

"Go right ahead," said Donatelli.

"You watch your mouth," growled Bud, grabbing Willie's arm. "After what you did in there tonight you oughta be down on your knees to that man, give you a way to save your gutless damn face—"

"Bud, leave him alone," said Donatelli.

"No chance, Vito," said Bud. Willie tried to jerk his arm loose, but the thin fingers tightened. "You never did know the difference between pain and injury, did you, Willie, you was always so—"

"Leave him alone," said Donatelli. He looked very tired.

Spoon raised his eyebrows at Jelly, who nodded and gently pushed Alfred and Henry toward the door. "We better go."

Out in the corridor, the guard touched Jelly's shoulder. "What's going on in there?"

"Nothing much."

"What's all the yelling?"

"Very painful stitches," said Spoon, his dark face expressionless.

"Oh."

The four of them walked toward a red exit sign. Spoon was shaking his head. "Too bad. Mr. Donatelli was really counting on Willie to go all the way."

"But it's just one defeat," said Henry.

"More than that," said Jelly. "Willie showed some dog tonight."

"Dog?" asked Alfred.

"It's true," said Spoon, stopping. "It was a bad cut, but if Willie had forgotten about it and kept pressing Becker he would have won, he might even have knocked him out in that round. But he got scared, it was the first time he had ever gotten hurt, really hurt, and he got scared. The way he concentrated on protecting that eye left him wide open, and Becker was sure to hurt him somewhere else. Mr. Donatelli saw that and stopped the fight, to save him from being hurt and to save him, I think, from showing himself a coward in front of the crowd. I can't think of another manager who would have done that."

"Me either," said Jelly. He grinned. "Same old Spoon. You're still giving lectures."

Spoon smiled and opened the exit door. "Sometimes I forget I'm not in front of a classroom."

A crowd of older men stood in front of the Garden, arguing about the fight. A workman on a ladder was pulling Willie Streeter's name off the marquee, letter by letter.

"I'm driving uptown," said Spoon. "Can I give anyone a lift?"

"Thanks," said Jelly, "but I got a girl friend lives around the corner and I promised to do her a favor tonight. She goes to cook and baker's school and I'm gonna check her homework."

"Same old Jelly Belly."

"I'm a growing boy, Spoon. I think these guys are going uptown. You know Henry Johnson, and this is a new tiger comin' around the gym. I don't even know his name."

"Alfred Brooks."

"Hi, I'm Bill Witherspoon." He shook hands with Henry and Alfred, and tapped the front of Jelly's pink shirt. "School's out in a few days, Horace. I'm coming up to the gym and see if I can whip some of that belly off you."

"All muscle," said Jelly. "Be good, men."

Spoon's car was an old blue Plymouth, and the three of them squeezed into the front. The back seat was covered with papers and books.

"Sorry you're so crowded," he said, moving the car into traffic, "but I'm studying for my permanent teacher's license and I've been collecting every scrap of paper I can get my hands on." He stopped for a light, and looked at Alfred. "Do you want to be a fighter?"

"I'm going to try," said Alfred. The light changed and Spoon looked away. Alfred watched the street lights play on Spoon's face. There were thin scars around his eyebrows, and two crossed blue scars on the bridge of his battered nose. "I saw your name on a fight poster up in the gym."

"Did you?" Spoon smiled out at the traffic. "For a while I was rated the Number Seven light-heavyweight contender."

Alfred leaned forward. "How come you quit?"

"It was very simple. One day, Mr. Donatelli said,

'Billy, I think it's time.' That's all he said. 'Billy, I think it's time.'"

"Why was that?"

"I was beginning to take too much punishment. I was winning, but I was starting to get hit regularly. This thing," he touched his nose, "was a big part of it. I argued, of course, but there isn't much point arguing with the boss unless you're right and he's just testing you. He told me he felt I should go back to college, full-time. I had taken a few courses at night. I had the money he made me save while I was going good, and I still had my eyesight and my hearing and my brain in one piece. I graduated from City College and I started substitute teaching. Last year I married a teacher. Mr. Donatelli was the best man." Spoon shrugged. "There I go, another speech. You fellows better tell me where to turn."

They rode the rest of the way in silence, Spoon driving carefully as the clean, well-kept buildings in the quiet white neighborhoods gave way to shabby houses on streets filled with black children and garbage. Once Henry whispered something to him, but Alfred let it go by—he was too busy winning the championship of the world, doing everything Mr. Donatelli told him to, never getting hurt or in trouble, smiling modestly down at Jelly and Spoon and Bud and Dr. Corey as the referee raised his arm.

"It's a long road, Alfred."

"Huh?" The car was parked in front of Henry's house, and Spoon was smiling at him.

"It's all right. I still have daydreams about what might have been." Spoon offered his hand. "Nice meeting you, Alfred, and seeing you again, Henry."

"You'll be coming up the gym?" asked Alfred.

"I'll be there. Good night."

"Good night. Thanks for the ride."

The car pulled away, and Henry tugged at his sleeve. "Want to sit on the stoop for a while?"

"I got to run tomorrow."

"Oh, yeah, that's right. Well, take it easy."

"Yeah."

Alfred took a few steps, then turned. "Henry?"

"Yeah?"

"Henry, I want to . . . uh, well, thanks a lot, Henry, you and your father too, for carrying me home that night."

Henry's thin face beamed. "Oh, sure, man, that's all right. You got KO'd, right? Can't win 'em all."

"Thanks."

He walked fast, in a hurry to get into bed and play the whole day back in his mind. The policemen on the corner raised their eyebrows at him, smiling and nodding like that, and the people on the stoop he waved to looked at each other, but Joe Louis had a good word for everybody and Sugar Ray and Cassius were men enough to be sweet. He started to say hello to the three boys standing in front of his stoop, but the word died in his throat when they turned around.

"Where you been, Uncle Alfred? We been waiting up all night for you," said Hollis.

"Now, let's us take a little walk," said Major, grabbing his arm.

Chapter 8

"Monday night and dressed so fine," said Major, leaning against the locked clubroom door.

"So fine," echoed Sonny, circling behind Alfred.

"Where you been, Uncle Alfred?"

Alfred stared at his black shoes. His knees were quivering. He wished he were sitting down.

Hollis showed his buck teeth. "You know Uncle Alfred can't talk 'less James is around to tell him what to say."

"Where's James?" asked Alfred.

"'Where's James, where's James?'" mimicked Major.

"What you want with me?"

"'What you want with me?'" mimicked Hollis.

"I'll tell you," snapped Major, pushing away from the door with his elbows. "Friday night we gonna hit Epsteins' again, only this time we're goin' in easy. This time, you gonna help us."

"No chance," said Alfred. The words were out of his mouth before he could swallow them back.

"What you say?" Major's eyes narrowed. "What you say to me?"

Alfred jammed his hands into his pockets, and pressed his fingers through the cloth into his thighs. His knees stopped quivering. "I said no."

"You said no?"

Alfred tensed for Major's attack, but there was only surprise on the heavy face.

"Look, slave, you don't have to come with us."

"No."

"All you got to do is disconnect them wires on the burglar alarm."

"No."

"Whatsa matter with you?" said Hollis.

"We'll split with you," said Major, "and you don't even have to come."

A vein popped out on Major's forehead, and his thick arms shook from the strain of keeping his muscles flexed. Where was all that coolness, that confidence? "No chance at all," Alfred said.

"You crazy?" asked Hollis, looking from Alfred to Major, then back to Alfred. "What's got to you?"

"I gotta go now," said Alfred, quivering again as he took a step toward the door.

Major jumped in front of him. "Where you think you going?"

"Home."

"Not till I let you." The knife came out fast and clicked open. "You ever hear of a squealer's scar?"

"Yeah."

"Then you know what I'm gonna do. One cut, from your mouth to your ear. You wear it the rest of your life."

Hollis was frozen, his mouth hanging slack. Sonny's eyes were dull and staring. Alfred pressed down on his toes to quiet his knees.

"You want the scar?"

"No."

"Then you're gonna do it, right?"

"No."

Major's tongue flicked out between his lips, and a bead of sweat broke out on his nose. "No?"

"He's crazy, Alfred's crazy, man," said Hollis.

"Must be crazy," said Major, straightening out of his knife-fighter's crouch. "I'll give you to Wednesday to get back to your senses."

"Answer's no," said Alfred.

"Don't have to decide now."

"I've decided now."

Major's voice was almost a scream. "But why?"

"Because I don't need to, that's why," said Alfred, taking a second step toward the door.

"The Epsteins don't care about you, you just a black nigger slave to them."

"Maybe so."

"Just a black boy to carry out their garbage, that's all."

"Got nothin' to do with them," said Alfred, moving past Major.

"You scared."

"You think that if you want." He put his foot on the first step.

"Why?"

He reached the door and unlocked it. "I got things to do, that's why."

"You got to Thursday to decide," screamed Major. "You got to Thursday—"

Alfred closed the door behind him just as his knees sagged, shuddering violently. Then he straightened, and all the way home he wanted to raise his right arm to the ringside crowd on the stoops.

Chapter 9

The birds were gossiping in the trees. There goes Alfred, smooth and easy, watch his knees come high and steady, cham-peen Alfred, looka him.

"Hang in there, Al, you're lookin' good," yelled the smaller cop, and Alfred waved back and put on a burst of speed just to show them how good he could look, his arms swinging easily at his sides, sucking in the air through his nostrils, letting it out his mouth. He ran for more than an hour, over grass and gravel, until the sun burned away the early mist and dried the dew. Squirrels skittered out of his way. Twice he saw other runners, and they waved and smiled at him. Like they were all partners. A stitch chewed at his side, but he kept running until the stitch disappeared. His breath caught in his ribs, but he kept running until he got his second wind. He didn't stop until cars and buses began to snarl and belch their way through the roads of the park, filling his nose and mouth with gas and oil fumes.

On the way home, he stopped every twenty steps for two quick deep-knee bends. He tried to hop up the first flight of stairs on his left leg and the second on his right. He almost made it.

At the door, he touched his toes ten times before throwing it open and striding smack into Aunt Pearl.

"Alfred?" Her face was stern, her hands on her hips.

"Yes, ma'am." He winked at the girls, kissed his aunt on top of her head, and cakewalked around the kitchen table. "No applause, folks, please."

"You drunk?"

"Now, Aunt Pearl, you know I never drink till after breakfast."

Charlene giggled in her cereal.

"Where you been?"

"Out running."

"From what?"

"From One Hundred Tenth to Eighty-fifth Street and back, nearly three miles."

"Don't you make fun of me, Alfred. Wipe that smirk off your face. Where you been?"

"Ladeez . . . and, uh, ladies. An announcement." The twins began to giggle too. "Introducing Alfred Brooks, the up-and-coming champeen of the world."

"Now you gonna be the down-and-out chump if you keep on." She snatched up a big wooden serving spoon. "You ain't that big I can't still whip that smirk off your face."

The girls ducked back into their cereal.

"Now. Where you been?"

"I been running in the park, build up my wind, get in shape, strengthen my legs—"

"Slow down. What are you talking about?"

"Aunt Pearl, I'm gonna be a boxer."

"Boxer!" The word rattled the cereal bowls, and the girls came up with milk on their noses. "Are you out of your mind? Boxer! Now you better . . . Alfred Brooks, I can tell, you're not fooling, are you?"

"No, ma'am. Mr. Donatelli. At the gym. He's gonna teach me to—"

"Boxer! And get your head busted open? What would your sweet momma say, Lord rest her soul, if she knew I let you . . ." Her voice trailed off. "Where you go last night?"

"Madison Square Garden."

"With who?"

"Henry and—"

"Henry Johnson?"

"Yeah. And Jelly Belly and Spoon—"

"Spoon?"

"Bill Witherspoon. He's a schoolteacher, used to be a boxer."

"Hmm." A trace of a smile tugged at the corners of her mouth. "An' I been so worried. First you get beat up, then act so strange yesterday morning. Then out so late last night and your good suit's all wrinkled, I thought you had some more trouble. An' this morning you sound like you're drunk or something."

"I feel good."

"Who's this Mr. Donatelli?"

"He's a boxing manager and he has a gym. Henry works there. He's had a couple champions."

"You planning to quit your job for this thing?"

"Not right away. Be a while before I get to be professional."

"I don't like this boxing business one bit. Full of gangsters, and people get hurt bad."

"Mr. Donatelli's no gangster. Last night he made Willie Streeter stop 'cause he had a cut eye, and he made Spoon quit 'cause he was getting hit too much. And Spoon was winning fights."

"We'll talk to Reverend Price about this. Now let's eat."

"I'll have orange juice, two boiled eggs, toast, and tea."

"You'll have what? This ain't a restaurant."

"Boxers can make big money, Aunt Pearl. You might not have to work no more, buy you a little house by Aunt Dorothy's, a car so you can drive to church on Sunday, a—"

"Don't you load no promises on your head, honey."

"I'm serious, Aunt Pearl."

"I know you are. You never been excited about anything in your life till today. But I just wish it was something else."

Chapter 10

Left . . . left . . . snap it out, Alfred, . . . left . . . right . . . right . . . left . . . left-left . . .

The first week was all pain, steel claws ripping at his shoulder muscles, raking his arms. The sweat rolled off his forehead and flooded his eyes, but they wouldn't let him stop to brush the sweat away . . . left . . . left . . . snap it out . . . even as his reflection grew hazy in the full-length mirror. Keep punching, they yelled, faster, harder, more.

"Your arms hurt, Alfred?"

"A little, Mr. Donatelli."

"They should hurt a lot. Okay, now. Time."

Time . . . time . . . three minutes of shadowboxing, one minute of rest, three minutes of shadowboxing, one minute of rest, time . . . time . . . until he woke up moaning one night, his arms as heavy as cement sacks, his fingers numb. Charlene was at the foot of the bed. She looked scared.

"Should I wake up Momma, Alfred?"

"No. Go on back to sleep. I had a bad dream."

"It musta been terrible."

Left . . . left . . . right . . . left . . . harder, harder, faster . . . snap it out, left . . . right . . . c'mon, c'mon . . .

The second week was worse. Bud yelled at him to stay up on the balls of his feet and Donatelli told him to keep his chin tucked against his chest.

Even Dr. Corey had his two cents worth: "Never take your eye off the peanut bag, Alfred."

Sit-ups, push-ups, deep-knee bends. Angel and

Jose, the Puerto Rican boys, cackled like hens when the medicine ball knocked him over like a tenpin. Denny grinned and threw it again harder, but Alfred was braced and ready. It only staggered him.

He could barely lift his arms up to his locker after workouts. Twice that week he fell asleep before dinner. At dawn, the alarm clock buzzed him awake like an angry rattlesnake.

That Sunday, after the morning service, Aunt Pearl marched him up to Reverend Price. She told him that Alfred needed guidance. He didn't like the way the Reverend looked down at him, scratching his big jaw, as if he were a school kid. But somewhere deep in his aching muscles a tiny voice was praying that Reverend Price would make him quit.

"What seems to be our problem, Sister Conway? Has Alfred strayed from the path of righteousness?"

"He's boxing, Reverend, he's—"

"Oh," said the preacher, his eyes moving around the room, his voice getting vague. "Youth is a time of great physical energy, Sister, and of curiosity. This is a passing phase. He'll soon grow tired of this meaningless pursuit and devote his . . ."

Left . . . left . . . faster, faster . . . atta boy . . . pick it up . . . chin in . . . right . . . right . . . snap it out . . .

By the middle of the third week the pain began to fade. He rushed through his exercises just to get in front of that mirror and shoot out those jabs, straight out, hard, until the little shocks in his shoulder told him the punches were straight and true. Spoon came up that week, and they all watched him spar a few rounds with the heavyweights, Jelly and Pete Krakover. Dr. Corey said that Spoon looked better than Willie Streeter did that night at the Garden.

Spoon worked with Alfred on the heavy bag,

showing him how to keep his wrist straight but relaxed so he could hit hard without hurting himself. But Spoon worked with Angel and Jose too, and there were some days when no one looked at him but Henry.

He started waking up before the alarm that week, fresher in the morning, stronger. The hour in the park was the best time of the day. It sometimes seemed as if he could run forever, showing his heels to the friendly policemen, waving at other runners. He wished he had someone to run with, someone like James, a partner, pacing him over the wet grass and over the gravel, sprinting across the deserted roadways, dropping back into a jog on the dirt paths. He'd even slow down for James. Someday, he thought, old James would come out from behind a tree, howling like Mosely of the Jungle, and he'd wink at Bad Brooks and fall into step. They had seen a movie like that once, two cowboy brothers who had a fight, and at the end they joined up again, riding into town together to face the gang. They won too.

The thought would make Alfred sad, and he'd speed up until he pushed it out of his mind. Henry was the nearest he had to a partner now, and Henry would never know how good it could feel when a running wind chilled the sweat in your hair.

At breakfast, Aunt Pearl would make some comment about his huge appetite, eating them out into the street, but she smiled when she said it. And then he went to work. Jake was still going to the bank in the afternoons, but Alfred couldn't get bothered about it, now when he felt his muscles flex every time he stacked the canned goods or lifted a box. Even the worst part of the job, carrying out the loaded garbage cans, didn't seem so bad when the muscles across his back and shoulders rippled and tensed. They had always rippled and tensed, but now even lugging garbage cans was part of training, of getting into shape.

There was a lull one afternoon. There were no customers in the store, and Alfred began throwing the hook at his reflection on the door of the steel food locker. He had just knocked out Jose, Angel, and Denny, one, two, three, when old Lou wandered into the back room.

"What's this, Alfred?"

"Sorry, Mr. Epstein, I was just—"

"From the shoulder it has to come, the power is here." He tapped a bony shoulder, shuffled his feet, and threw a slow but graceful left hook. "You want to be a boxer?"

"Yes. I'm training at Donatelli's gym."

"A good man, Donatelli. Ask him about Lou Epstein someday."

"Hey! Are you Lightning Lou Epp?"

"How did you know?"

"Bud Martin talked about you. He said you were real good, but you cut too easy."

A slow smile spread across Lou's thin face. "He remembered, eh? A good cut man, Bud Martin, one of the best. How long you been training?"

"About three weeks."

"Forget it. I would tell my own son the same thing, especially my own son. Forget it."

"Why?"

Lou sat down on a packing case. He rubbed a small red sore on the top of his bald head. "Why? I'll tell you, Alfred. Once it was something, boxing. There were dozens of fight clubs in the city. You could see a good fight every night of the week. Irish fighters, Italian, Jewish fighters, then Negro fighters, there were enough matches for anybody who wanted to fight. No more. Even a good fighter can't make a living out of it. You know why?"

"People aren't interested in going to fights?"

"Part of it," said Lou. "Television came in, and used the same fighters over and over again, a few got rich, the rest had to get jobs. And even the rich ones lost their money. The racketeers, the crooked matchmakers, the rotten managers just—"

"Mr. Donatelli's not like that, he—"

"Sure, sure," said Lou, raising a spidery hand. "Donatelli's one in a million. That's why he has to sleep in a room by the gym. Boxing people don't like to do business with an honest man. And another thing, the kids these days aren't interested in learning to fight. It's hard work. Nobody wants to work no more. Who knows, maybe they're right."

He stood up. "You see that friend of yours, James Mosely, anymore?"

"Not since . . . not for a long time."

"Okay. You tell Bud hello for me, Donatelli, too."

Off your heels . . . faster . . . left, right, left, right . . . snap it out, jab, hook, jab . . . harder . . .

He began to lose track of the days. They rolled off like perspiration, up at dawn, run, breakfast, work, the gym, home, dinner, television, sleep. Sometimes on Fridays or Saturdays he went to the movies with Henry and Jelly, but it wasn't like going to the movies with James. Henry just sat there, his mouth open, staring at the screen, and Jelly was always jumping up for candy or ice cream. Not like the old days when Alfred would follow James up to a corner of the balcony and root for the monster and cheer the Indians and afterward change the ending of the picture if they didn't like how it came out.

In late July, Aunt Pearl went to the Elversen's summer house and left the girls in Queens with Dorothy and Wilson. The apartment seemed large and empty. Now he could sleep late on Sundays. Sometimes he slept right through the day, getting up only to eat and doze in front of the television set.

Then Monday and dawn and the alarm clock.

The peanut bag was easy, once he got the rhythm he could stand under it all day, making it sound like a machine gun. Henry would watch him, grinning, as if he was really doing something, but Donatelli would walk by without even looking. Alfred could hear the manager think. The bag doesn't have any arms to hit you back with.

"Real good speed on the bag, Alfred," said Henry.

"Anybody can do that," said Alfred.

Henry looked away.

Left . . . left . . . hook, shift, hook, jab, right . . .

"Open your mouth," said Dr. Corey one day, shoving in a white plastic mouthpiece. "When you're ready for your first fight, I'll make you a custom-fitted one."

"Aaaargh." Alfred gagged and spat it out. Jelly slapped his knee, and Denny laughed.

"Again," said Dr. Corey.

"I can't breathe."

"You'll have to breathe through your nose."

"Quick, sharp breaths," said Spoon. "In, out, in, out, that's the way."

He gagged for half an hour, but then he got it, and went back to the mirror, up on the balls of his feet, quick little steps, forward on the jab, sideways for the hook, da-da-dum-dum, quick and easy.

"Time," called Donatelli, passing by. "Your footwork's coming along, but this is no dancing class. Snap that jab out, harder . . . harder . . ."

And when the workout was over and every muscle shrieked, there was nothing like standing under the shower, the hot water drowning all the ache, closing your eyes and tilting your face up into it.

"Whaddya, drinking it, Alfred? C'mon, there are five guys out here waiting to get in."

He ran into Major one night as he was coming home from the gym.

"Hey, Alfred, how you been?"

"Okay."

"Don't run off, man, wait a minute. We never see you 'round the clubroom no more."

"Been busy."

"Yeah, I heard you're working out. Say, man, you're not still sore about that little misunderstanding we had. I was just trying you out."

"Sure."

"Well, come around," said Major.

"Sure."

"I mean it. James comes by once in a—"

"James around?" said Alfred.

"Sometimes. I'll let you know."

"Do that."

Willie Streeter came back to the gym, sullen and overweight. Donatelli took him to a training camp in the mountains for ten days to try to get him in shape for an out-of-town fight. The temperature in the gym sometimes reached 101 degrees and everyone started snapping at each other. One day, Pete Krakover threw a boxing shoe at Jelly.

"Use your own trunks, fat meat."

Jelly looked up from the locker bench, his body slick with sweat, his mouth sucking air like a fish's gill.

"What?"

"You heard me, fat meat. Use your own damn trunks."

"What I want with your stinking Polack trunks?"

"You black tub a lard," yelled Pete, rushing forward on floppy shower clogs. Jelly stood up to meet him, hands up.

Jose and Angel danced between them, a step ahead of Bud Martin.

"He no wear your trunks, Petey," yelled Angel.

"He too fat," yelled Jose.

"I sent 'em all out to be washed," said Bud.

Pete grinned sheepishly. "Sorry, Jelly."

"The heat, man," said Jelly, plopping back down. "You ain't used to it. Always snows in Poland."

"I never been there," said Pete. "My grandmother says it's beautiful in the summer, green and warm."

"No kidding?"

Snap it out . . . snap it out . . . snap it out . . .

"Time," called Henry. "You're just pushing that jab, Alfred, you got to throw it."

"Why don't you try?" snarled Alfred. "I'm sorry, Henry, I didn't mean it."

"That's okay," said Henry. "Time."

Time, time, time, thought Alfred, flicking out the jab. I can do this in my sleep. Across the gym, Spoon and Bud were watching Angel and Jose spar in the ring. They were both turning pro soon. Jelly and Pete were waiting to go in next. He looked up at the weight chart over the scale. Six weeks, six damn weeks, gained six pounds and never punched anybody except my own face in the mirror. I'm not even an amateur yet.

"Time," said Henry. "What's the matter, Alfred?"

"Nothing's the matter."

"You sure?"

"Sure."

"Okay. Time."

Donatelli came back on a Friday, his thin lips tight. Willie had lost his out-of-town fight. The manager spent the afternoon leaning on the ring ropes, watching Jose and Angel spar. Alfred threw out his jab mechanically, staring at the back of the square, white-topped head, willing it to turn around and look at him. The head didn't move.

"Hey, man, you're looking sharp," said Major, swaggering into mirror view.

"Let's go, snap it out," said Henry.

"Got any fights comin' up, man?"

"C'mon, Alfred, keep punching, left . . . left . . ."

Alfred dropped his arms and turned around. "No, I'm just—"

Bud Martin tapped Major on the shoulder. "That boy's working. You can talk to him later, outside." He jerked a thumb toward the door.

"Okay, baby," said Major. "Come on around, Alfred. Little party tonight. James gonna be up."

He swaggered across the gym, rolling his big shoulders, stopping only to rap the peanut bag on his way out.

"You and Major tight now?" asked Henry.

"No."

"Wonder what he wants."

"Just being friendly."

"I'll bet," said Henry. "Time."

He threw out his arms mechanically, left, right, left, right, but there were no shocks in his shoulders, just a dull ache along the ridge muscles of his back. Do this in my sleep, he thought.

"Time," said Donatelli. He shook his head. "You're not doing anything at all today, Alfred. You're not concentrating. Is anything the matter?"

"No."

"You've got to work harder."

"Yeah."

Donatelli nodded and strolled away, over to the heavy bag. He put one hand on Jelly's shoulder and one on Pete's and all three of them laughed at something Jelly said. Come on back here, thought Alfred, come on back. Show me something, tell me I'm gonna spar someday, put on a pair of real gloves.

"Time," said Henry.

"Time out," said Alfred. He walked to his locker, peeling off the wet gym clothes. Too hot today. Too damn hot.

He showered and dressed quickly. Henry was waiting for him at the door.

"You want to go to the movies tonight?"

"No."

"Triple feature, be fun. Jelly says if the monster don't win tonight he's gonna tear the movie house down."

"I said no."

"You going to the clubroom?"

"I don't know."

"You're in training, Alfred, you better not—"

"I can take care of myself."

He walked quickly down the steps, the long, steep, dirty steps. He wondered if Donatelli was just too cheap to fix them. A guy could break his neck.

The street was still hot, even with the sun sliding out of sight. Music blared out of open windows. Kids clattered up and down the gutter. Friday night. On every street corner people lounged and stared, waiting for something to happen. Cars cruised up and down. Men brought out the tables for cards and dominoes. Go home to an empty house, eat dinner, watch television, go to sleep early like every other night. Too hot to sleep, he thought. Sleep for what?

To run tomorrow and shadowbox and count out your life in sit-ups?

He headed toward the clubroom. Wonder what James is doing these days. Never even called me back. Still mad about that burglar alarm. Straighten that out. Just drop in for a little while. See what's happening.

Chapter 11

Major saw him first. "There's the champ."

"Hey, champ," said Sonny.

"It's my main man, Alfred," said Major, throwing an arm around his shoulders and pulling him down into the darkened clubroom. "What's your drink, brother?"

"I'm in training," said Alfred. A single red bulb shone over the spinning record player. He squinted at the shadowy figures in the room, some dancing, others sprawled on floor pillows. "Where's James?"

"He'll be by. Wine?"

"No, thanks."

"Take a night off, man, you're in shape. Gotta have some kicks."

Major's girl, June, came out of the shadows. "You come alone, Alfred?"

"Yes."

"Good," she said, linking her arm in his. "Got somebody I want you to meet."

"Can't stay long."

"Wait till you meet her." She led him across the floor, weaving among the dancers, stepping over couples whispering and necking. She lit a match, and a dark, chubby girl with a curly, blond wig and thick, pink lipstick smiled up at Alfred.

"This is Arlene," said June. The match went out, and June let his arm go.

"I'm Alfred Brooks."

"Hi."

"Dance?"

He was surprised at how easily she came into his arms, so close that the strong, sweet smell of her perfume made him dizzy in the heat of the crowded room. The music was low, funky blues, and he swayed to it.

"You live near here?"

She shook her head, and the stiff hairs of the wig brushed his nose. "I'm visiting June. She's my cousin."

Major came around with the wine bottle, and Arlene drank from it. Alfred pushed it away, twice, when Major pressed it against his chest. Then he came back with half an orange soaked in vodka.

"This is good for you, man."

Why not, Alfred thought. He sucked on it, feeling new heat rise out of his empty stomach into his head. The party became a blur, a sweet, sticky blur, Major left the wine bottle with him, and Alfred and Arlene danced into a corner. Someone began pounding conga drums.

Hollis swam by, and punched his arm. "Good to see ya, Alfred."

"Yeah. James come in?"

"Not yet."

"You sure he's coming?"

Hollis patted a jacket pocket. "You can be sure he's coming."

"Who's James?" asked Arlene.

"A guy I know," said Alfred. "Let's sit down awhile."

Someone began passing a cigarette around, and the way everyone dragged on it he knew it was marijuana. Alfred shook his head when Arlene put it between his lips.

"It'll relax you, honey," she said, stroking the back of his neck, and he inhaled.

The red bulb burned out, and it was pitch-dark in the clubroom. The wine bottles kept coming around, and the cigarettes. Except for soft laughter, the music covered all sound in the room. Like a nice dark movie, he thought. He took longer pulls on the bottle, and deeper drags on the cigarette to keep the warm, soft feeling in his head. Once the door opened for some newcomers, and he saw Arlene smiling up at him, her face puffy, the blond wig tipped over one eye.

At dawn, an invisible fist slammed into his stomach, and he barely made it out to the alley. He leaned against a brick wall and tried to catch his breath. Newspaper pages fluttered along the street on a morning breeze. He saw a patch of pink sky between the buildings. For a moment he thought about the park, the good feeling of gravel underfoot and the wind streaming past his face. Then he went back down the basement steps.

Sonny had passed out on the couch, and Hollis' date was slumped over the mop sink. Hollis was dancing with Arlene. There was just a little bit of wine left, and they passed it around, trying to get the nighttime glow started in the dirty glare of rising daylight. Some new people came with bottles wrapped in brown paper bags, and Major blacked out the little basement window with his jacket. The party started all over again.

"Hey, Alfred," mumbled Major, pulling him away from Arlene. "Your man."

"James."

The round face was thin, the eyes sunken. His suit seemed too big for him.

"Where you been, James?"

"Lil Unca Alfid," said James. His teeth were yellow.

"Where you been, James?"

"I been 'round."

"Never called or nothing."

"What for?"

"We were partners, remember, we . . ." He felt dizzy, and shook his head. "James, I forgot about that burglar alarm. Honest. I didn't mean for you to—"

"It don't matter now."

"Does. Don't want you thinking—"

"I know you didn't mean nothing, you never mean nothing. You just fool enough to forget about that alarm." He turned his back on Alfred.

Major came over and put an arm around James' neck. "Hollis got something for you, brother."

The clubroom began to tilt for Alfred, but he took a deep breath and grabbed the back of a chair. Hollis pulled a packet of white powder out of his jacket pocket. Alfred stumbled over.

"No, James, you don't wanna mess with that stuff, you don't wanna—"

"Go 'way, Unca Alfid." James was almost snarling.

"No good, James," mumbled Alfred, feeling the room sway.

James took the packet and began fumbling with it. Alfred followed him into a corner, trying to clear his head, steady himself. "You and me, James, partners."

"That was kid stuff," said James as his fingers, trembling, tore at the packet.

"Listen to me, James, please." Alfred leaned against the tilting wall, his legs buckling, his eyes fogging.

"What you got to say?" asked James, suddenly staring at Alfred, waiting as Alfred's lips moved without any sound.

He tried to clear his head, to think, to answer

James' question, but the floor came up and sent him sprawling. James looked down at him, shook his head, and went back to his white powder.

Chapter 12

Far, far away, the rattlesnake was buzzing, short bursts, time to run, time to run, time, time, screamed Henry, but Jelly Belly was sitting on his head. Jose and Angel, chattering in Spanish, were jumping on his stomach. Mr. Donatelli was sitting on his legs shouting, shift your weight, shift your weight. Then they all disappeared and left him alone, lying on the linoleum kitchen floor in a pool of ice-cold sweat. The telephone was ringing. He crawled over to it and fumbled with the receiver. The phone crashed to the floor.

"Yeah?"

"Alfred?"

"Aunt Pearl?"

"You all right, Alfred? You sound so strange."

"All right."

"I can't hear you."

"Just woke up."

"It's nine-thirty, Alfred."

"Slept late."

"It's nine-thirty at night."

"Uh, went to sleep early. Training."

"That's good. Now listen, Alfred, Mrs. Elversen's gonna need me to stay up here till Thursday.

"Okay."

"You still there, Alfred?"

"Yeah."

"Now you call Dorothy in the morning, before they go to church. Tell her I'll pick up the girls Thursday night. You got that?"

"Thursday night."

"Right. There's no answer there now, they must be at the movies. You sure you're all right, Alfred?"

"Fine and dandy."

"Now don't forget, Alfred."

"Thursday night."

"Right. Bye, now."

"Bye."

He stumbled into the front room and turned on the televisions set. He passed out before the picture appeared.

He woke once to go to the bathroom, and a cowboy was standing on top of a speeding stagecoach, shooting Indians. He passed out again in the bathroom. When he dragged himself back, the television was humming behind a flickering test pattern. He fell into the couch.

He awoke to organ music. There was a picture of Jesus in long white robes on the screen, and the words "Dawn Devotional" under His feet. Vaguely he remembered that he had to call Dorothy about something, but his body was fastened to the couch. His arms were too heavy to lift. The conga drums were pounding in his head. It seemed like hours before he was able to lift his head, hours more before he could move his arms and legs. Slowly he stood up. The organ music was swelling. He staggered into the kitchen. The clock on the cabinet was ticking off the last few seconds to seven o'clock. With hands as clumsy as boxing gloves, he fumbled a pot out of the stove and filled it with water. He dozed while it boiled away. The smell of the burning pot jerked him awake. He started all over again, spilling the instant coffee powder. It was nearly eight before he had the black coffee in a cup. It was hot and bitter, but it washed away the sandy cotton in his mouth.

The telephone rang.

"You ready, champ?"

"What?"

"Got us a car, Alfred. We're going out to Coney Island, remember?"

"Major?"

"Yeah, man. Be in front of the house in five minutes."

"Don't feel right."

"Ocean air, champ, best thing for you."

"No, I—" Major hung up.

A wave of sickness washed up from his stomach.

"*Good morning, Kiddie Klubbers, it's Uncle Harry—*"

He rushed in and snapped off the set just as a fat man with a false nose began pouring corn flakes into the screen.

Alfred made more coffee. He gulped it black and boiling. Mr. Donatelli said never have more than one cup a day, if that much. Smart-meat Donatelli, knows all. I oughta call him up and get a program for hangovers. Outside, a car horn sounded short, sharp blasts. He poured a third cup of coffee. Someone pounded on the door.

"Hollis?"

"We're waitin' on you, Alfred."

"Look, I'm—"

"C'mon, man, you need a break. Been workin' too hard."

Alfred let Hollis lead him downstairs.

On the street, Major waved him into the red-leather front seat of a white Cadillac convertible. Hollis climbed into the back with Sonny and a younger boy Alfred had seen around the neighborhood.

"Who's car is this?"

"Mine," said Major, jerking it away from the curb with a screech of gears. "Loaned it off a guy."

They cruised along the streets, past families dressed for church and winos stumbling out of alleys into the bright morning sunlight. Major lounged behind the wheel, guiding the big car with the fingertips of his right hand. His left arm dangled out, slapping the door in time to music blaring from the car radio.

"Now this is something, ain't it?" He grinned at Alfred.

"Yeah."

Major took his hand off the wheel and plucked a pair of tinted sunglasses out of his T-shirt pocket. While he was slipping them on, the car veered toward a young couple crossing the street. They scrambled back to the sidewalk.

"Wake up," yelled Major, laughing, grabbing the wheel and straightening the car.

People watched the Cadillac cruise past. Look at them wish themselves into the car, Alfred thought, phony cats with long-playing records under their arms and no machine to play them on. Just hanging around, waiting for something to happen. He leaned back into the red leather.

The car picked up speed, swinging onto a highway. Off to the right, the Hudson River lay blue-green and quiet, glinting under the sun. Small boats churned through the water.

"Now there's some living," said Hollis, leaning forward.

"I'll loan one of them sometime," said Major.

"Hear there's some real parties on those boats," said Hollis.

"You ever know a black man got one of them?" asked Major.

"No."

"They won't let you park it," said Major. "Even if you bought one, you couldn't park it, just have to keep goin' up and down the river. They don't get you one way, they get you another. Right, Alfred?"

"If you say so."

Major laughed. "You all right, Alfred."

The highway narrowed into a tunnel, and Major yelled, "Toll booth." He stretched his left arm toward the back seat.

"Got no change, Major," said the younger boy, "only dollar bills."

"They take dollar bills," said Major. He slowed for the toll booth, took the boy's dollar, and paid. He pocketed the change.

Coney Island was hot and noisy, the streets off the boardwalk choked with boys and girls, white and black, marching up and down, looking each other over. Alfred began to feel cramps in his stomach at the mingled smells of cotton candy, barbecue, fried chicken, and hot dogs. He realized that he hadn't eaten since Friday lunch, nearly two full days ago. He heard distant screams from the thundering roller coaster. Up ahead, a huge Ferris wheel spun slowly against the blue sky.

Major double-parked in front of an outdoor stand. "Go and get some food, Justin. Dogs, French fries, some a that sweet corn. You go help him carry it, Sonny."

"Carry it," said Sonny, climbing out.

"Mustard on the dogs, Major?" asked Justin.

"Everything on the dogs."

Major leaned back in the seat, his arms behind his head. "We'll get us some food, then go find us some pretty little foxes. You got that bottle, Hollis?"

"Cops," said Hollis.

Major and Alfred turned. Two policemen were moving toward them, checking drivers' licenses and registration papers along the row of double-parked cars.

"Don't need that," said Major, starting the car.

"You steal this car?" asked Alfred.

"Gonna return it," said Hollis, "we just . . ."

His words were lost in the sudden roar of the engine. Major jerked the car into traffic. The policemen began to run, shouting, as Major stomped on the accelerator and pounded the horn at people crossing the street. A baby carriage rolled up in front of the car, and Major slammed on the brakes.

"Let's get out a here."

Alfred vaulted over the door, into the gutter, landing hard on his right foot. The ankle twisted under him and he went to his knees, but he got up and plunged into the crowd on the sidewalk, pushing through. Keep moving, keep moving. He ducked his head at the police whistle, and rounded a corner, slamming into a hard chest, and a hand cuffed him on the head. Keep moving, and then he was on the boardwalk, and he slowed down, the ankle beginning to throb, and he let himself be carried along in the flowing crowd. He walked until every step on his right foot sent a shaft of pain up through his ankle. He sat down on a bench.

Thousands of people were jammed together on the beach. He could hardly see the sand. Men and women lay stretched out on blankets and umbrellas, slowing down and sucking in their stomachs whenever they passed girls. Babies cried over the noise of transistors. He started walking again, until he found a food stand. He bought spare ribs, buttered corn, French fries, and a Pepsi-Cola. Worst things you can eat, said Donatelli. Alfred gobbled it down as fast as he could. A moment later he was hanging over the boardwalk rail, vomiting.

"Disgusting," said a voice behind him.

"Poor kid."

"A junkie, tryin' to beat it with food, just can't do it, you just can't . . ."

He got away from there as fast as his ankle would let him, stumbling along with the crowd. Shoes kicked at the back of his feet whenever he slowed down. His body itched from streaming sweat. His shirt and pants were damp. He got off the boardwalk, and limped along the strange Brooklyn streets. Every time he passed a policeman he lowered his head and held his breath.

He found a movie house along a wide avenue and went right inside without bothering to find out what was playing. The theater was cool and his stomach quieted down. He bought an ice cream cup and pressed the frosty paper container against his cheeks and temples until the fever in his face disappeared. The ice cream melted, and it went down easily and stayed down. He had another, and began to feel better.

He watched the movie. Handsome, well-dressed white men got in and out of fancy cars with beautiful blond women. For a while, he tried to follow the picture, then gave it up. You all right, Alfred. Thanks, Major, thanks a lot. How long ago now, a month, two months? The last time Major used his fists and feet to bust me up. This time he . . . Don't blame him, man, he didn't pour all that stuff into you at the party. You did that. He didn't put a knife in your throat and make you take a ride. You got in the car. Major was just being friendly. I'll bet, said Henry. If they don't get you one way, they get you another.

He stumbled, blinking, back into the hot street. It

was like walking through an invisible curtain. He walked for a long time before he found a subway station. On the platform, people moved away from him, wrinkling their noses. He noticed there was dried vomit on his sneakers.

It was early evening before he got back to Harlem. The nationalist speakers were on their stepladders, screaming into the dying sun. "Tomorrow morning, Monday morning, you wake up, check the baby to see if the rats bit its ears off—"

"You said it, brother."

"—then you go on down to meet The Man . . ."

"Brooksy, hey, Brooksy, wanna talk to you. Heard you been . . ." He crossed the street, not even bothering to pretend that he hadn't heard Harold. I heard you, smart meat, now get lost. This happy little darky just ain't interested.

He walked aimlessly for hours. His ankle throbbed again, but he kept moving. Hungry-eyed faces filled the street corners, waiting for something to happen. Only a few hours left in the weekend, brother. If the action don't come, it'll be another five days before you can get back on your street corner and start waiting again.

He suddenly realized he was on the familiar block of low apartment buildings, a store-front church, a delicatessen, a pawn shop, and on the corner, a bar. The door leading upstairs was slightly open, as usual. A dim light flickered through the dirty plate-glass window on the third floor. He stared at it for a long time. Then he went home.

The telephone was ringing as he came through the door.

"Where you been, Alfred?"

"Major."

"Thought they got you."

"No, I—"

"Listen, man, I don't think there's gonna be no trouble, but if anybody asks where you was today, we all was over your house playin' cards. Got that?"

"Playin' cards."

"Right. You doin' anything now?"

"Yeah." He hung up.

He filled the bathtub with hot water, and stripped off his shoe and sock. The ankle was swollen and soft to the touch. He sat on the edge of the tub and soaked his foot. Couldn't run tomorrow if I wanted to, he thought. As if I wanted to. Knock your brains out, bust your back, run your feet down to the bone. What for? The Man said, nothing's promised you. We know that.

He lay on his aunt's bed with his clothes on, and closed his eyes. It seemed as if it was only a minute later when they opened again. A pink dawn. Running time. His ankle was a little stiff, but the swelling was gone. No pain. He started up, then lay back. Don't need that foolishness. Ain't gonna be a boxer anyway. Run for nothing. The birds are gonna have to get along without old Alfred.

Ben Epstein winked at him when he came into the store. "How was your weekend, Alfred?"

"Real fine."

"One long party, eh?"

"You know."

The day dragged on and on. He sorted the new crates, stacked the canned goods, lugged the filthy garbage pails out back. His muscles felt sore. He went straight home after work and opened a can of pork and beans. He didn't bother to cook it. Cold and greasy, each spoonful dropped to the pit of his stomach and lay there. The phone rang.

"You all right, Alfred?"

"Aunt Dorothy?"

"Just talked to Pearl, she was surprised you didn't call us yesterday. Not like you, Alfred."

"I'm sorry. I forgot."

"All that exercising must really tire you out. Come on out to dinner tomorrow night, been so long since you been here."

"Well, maybe—"

"Jeff's here, you could talk with Jeff and—"

"I'm sorry, Aunt Dorothy, I got something else to do."

"You're going to wear yourself out, all that exercising and running. Take a break and come on out. Jeff won't be home again till Thanksgiving."

"I can't."

"Well, you know you're always welcome."

"Thanks."

He went into the front room and stretched out on the couch. That's all I got to do, go listen to Jeff count up all his opportunities for advancement. Take a break. Hollis said that too. Yeah, I'll take a break. About this time Old Uncle Alfred would be beating at the air in front of a mirror or skipping rope. Like a fool. Good thing nobody ever looked at me much up in that gym or they'd fall over laughing.

He turned on the television and watched it until he couldn't keep his eyes open. Then he slept.

Tuesday dragged along too.

"That must of been some weekend," said Ben, winking.

"Sure."

Late in the afternoon, while he was sweeping the storeroom, he saw Henry limp in through the front door. Alfred quietly slipped out the back door and waited until Henry left. Why can't people just leave you alone, he thought.

He didn't feel like going back to the empty apartment after work. He walked. He passed the clubroom and quickened stride. If I just could have talked James into going to a movie that Friday night. If I just could have thought of something to say at the party when he was looking at me with the junk in his hand. Some partner I am.

He found a triple feature up on 125th Street, and went in. He had seen all the pictures on television already. So what. See them again, see them a thousand times, the new ones are the same as the old ones anyway.

He came out into the night. There weren't too many people on the street. Tomorrow is Wednesday, a working day. Get up, go to work, go home and sleep so you can work some more and pay for your fun on the weekend. And then it's Monday again. Days move so slow. The stores along the avenue were already advertising back-to-school clothes. The summer went so fast. Where'd the summer go? In the park, up in the gym. He walked faster. What makes you think you won't quit this too, Mr. Donatelli said. Smart meat.

He looked up. A dim light flickered through the dirty plate-glass window. How'd I get here? Habit, he thought. He started to walk past the sagging door. Maybe go up for a minute. Might as well clean out the locker.

He took the old steps one at a time, twice stopping to catch his breath. Last time I have to go up these crummy steps. Donatelli was sitting on a folding chair, tipped back, staring out the window. He didn't turn around.

Slowly Alfred stuffed his sweat shirts, trunks, supporters, socks, his secondhand boxing shoes into a paper shopping bag. Maybe I can sell them back to

Bud Martin for some new kid who would really use them. He felt tears in his eyes. He looked at the square head, silhouetted against the flickering neon lights. Turn around, turn around. If you don't look now, you never going to see me again. He slammed the locker shut. The clang echoed through the room. The head didn't turn.

At the door, Alfred said, "Good-bye, Mr. Donatelli."

The head barely moved. "Good-bye. Good luck to you."

"Well . . . So long. Thanks."

"You're welcome."

"I'm sorry."

"You've got nothing to apologize to me for."

"Mr. Donatelli?"

"Yes."

"If . . . if I had kept going, would I ever have got any good?"

"Who knows?"

"If . . . if I had wanted to, would I have . . . you know, been a contender?"

"Don't ask me."

"Then who?" said Alfred.

"Yourself. Anyone can be taught how to fight. A contender, that you have to do yourself."

"If I wasn't giving it up, would I ever have got a chance to spar?"

"Probably."

"To have a real fight someday?"

"Perhaps."

"Would you know then?"

"Maybe."

"Maybe? Only maybe?" The head didn't move. "When would you know?"

"When you got hurt in the ring for the first time,

really hurt. Then I would know."

"Would you . . ." He let the shopping bag drop. "Will you tell me then? When you know?"

"I won't have to, Alfred. You'll know, too."

Chapter 13

Left . . . left . . . snap it out . . . drive in . . . mix it up . . . don't let 'im get away, Alfred . . . press . . .

Angel kept slipping Alfred's jab. He cocked his head at the last possible instant and grinned as Alfred's gloved fist shot harmlessly over his shoulder. And each time Alfred missed, Angel belted him in the stomach. There was no pain, only anger that drove his teeth deeper into the mouthpiece. The air exploded out of his nostrils and sweat ran into his eyes. He closed his eyes and swung wildly, and Angel, laughing, belted the side of his headguard.

"Time," called Henry.

"You're not workin' your combinations," said Bud, pulling out the mouthpiece. "You been throwin' one punch at a time and that's no good."

"But, I—"

"Time," called Henry, and Bud shoved the mouthpiece back in.

Jab-jab-hook . . . jab-hook-right . . . jab . . . hook to the body . . . cross to the chin . . . body . . . head . . . jab . . . jab . . . jab . . .

August, gasping for breath, melted into September. It was cooler in the park at dawn now. But it was hot in the gym, always hot in the gym, the leather headguard squeezing his temples, the metal protective cup pinching his thighs. The 16-ounce sparring gloves felt like lead pillows. Angel slipped the jab, and Denny slipped the jab, while Henry screamed and Bud yelled, and sometimes Donatelli watched and sometimes he didn't.

When Alfred remembered his dreams the next morning, they were always the same: A fly was sitting on the tip of his nose, and every time he reached to brush it away he saw he had no hands.

"Ten seconds left," called Henry.

Angel's face, framed in the headguard, bobbed up, mocking him. Last chance for today, thought Alfred. Now. He snapped out a left jab, straight at the moving head, just as he had for weeks. And Angel, as he had for weeks, cocked his head and let it shoot by, never bothering to watch Alfred's shuffling feet. Angel didn't see the right until it was almost too late. When he jerked his head away from the right, a left hook slammed into his face.

Angel's head snapped backwards, his face twisted with surprise. His gloves automatically flew up to his face. Alfred dropped his right shoulder, took a quick step forward on his right foot, and slammed a short right uppercut into Angel's belly.

Alfred plunged forward, the months of shadowboxing taking over now, left . . . left . . . right to the face . . . hook . . . and Angel was reeling against the ropes, a drop of blood oozing from his nose.

"Time," called Bud. Jelly clapped. Pete leaned over the ropes and slapped his shoulder.

"You're thinking," said Donatelli. "Not bad."

Not bad, thought Alfred, spitting the mouthpiece into Henry's hand. That's like a medal from anyone else.

Jose began unlacing Angel's gloves. "Alfred really catch you one, ay?"

"I do it so he feel good," said Angel.

"Nex' time he feel so good he knock you out," said Jose, winking at Alfred. Angel began chattering in machine-gun Spanish.

"You did real good," said Henry, unlacing Alfred's

gloves. "That was the best hook you ever threw."

"I'm not sure I know what I did right."

"You been taking a little step before you threw the hook, made you off balance. This time, you pivoted. Like this." Henry threw a slow hook, and pivoted on his left leg. The crippled leg.

"Yeah," said Alfred, practicing it. "Yeah. How'd you know?" He tried to keep his eyes from staring down at Henry's leg.

"I'm learning too, man," said Henry. Then he noticed Alfred's stare, and limped heavily away.

Stick and move . . . in and out . . . jab-jab-right . . . jab-jab-hook . . . jab-hook-right . . . mix 'em up . . . press . . . press . . .

Denny's hands were quick, but his footwork was slow. Stand and fight with him, he'll spin your head around. Stick and move, he doesn't have a chance. Sorry, Denny, thought Alfred, my head's not a punching bag for you.

"Time," called Bud.

"You have nice moves, Alfred, very nice moves."

"Mr. Epstein!"

Old Lou smiled. "I have to hear from the neighborhood how good you're getting? So I came up to see."

"Hey, Lightning," said Bud, raising his fists. "You ain't been up for years."

"Don't talk about years. How's my boy doing?"

"Gettin' there, he's gettin' there. You look good, Lou, ready to go ten."

"Ten steps, maybe."

"Sure." Bud clapped him on the shoulders. "Saw Kid Ryan last week, he was askin' for you."

"A rematch I won't give him, even after forty years. A tough one, remember that night . . ."

When Alfred came out of the shower, Bud and Lou

were throwing slow, creaky punches in the air, and laughing. He was dressed and half out the door when Lou called, "Wait just a minute, Alfred."

Lou took a little black purse from his pocket, counted out some bills, and pressed them into Bud's hand. "Don't tell Ryan where it comes from, pride he always had."

"Thanks," said Bud. "Take it easy, Lou."

"How else can I take it?" He put a hand on Alfred's shoulder, bracing himself as they walked slowly down the steps.

On the street, Lou said, "You didn't take my advice."

"Well, Mr. Epstein, I—"

"You should have your own mind, do what you want. Ben tells me it takes you half the time to sort the new stock Monday mornings. How come you suddenly have more energy now?"

"Well, I—"

"Let me figure it out, I have to keep my mind active. You know how to work the register?"

"No. But I could learn."

"Sure you could learn. Maybe come in a little early tomorrow, before we get busy. I'll show you some things."

"Thanks, Mr. Epstein, I'll—"

"Don't thank me, Alfred. I'm not giving you anything you won't have to work for."

Stick and move . . . double-jab . . . double-hook . . . cross with the right . . . hook over the jab . . . slip and stick . . . break clean . . . move 'im, Alfred.

Jose was not as fast as Angel or Denny, but he hit harder. Twice, he fired straight rights through Alfred's guard, stinging, rib-bruising rights that took Alfred's breath away. It wasn't until the third sparring round that Alfred timed the rhythm of Jose's attack, and dropped his left arm, catching the right on his elbow. Jose's face was unprotected and Alfred pumped a fast right into his mouth. He pivoted on his left foot, and threw the hook in a smooth, short arc. Jose dropped like a sack of potatoes. He was back on his feet immediately, but Donatelli jumped into the ring and grabbed Alfred's gloves.

"Better go downstairs," he said softly. "It's time you were fitted for that custom-made mouthpiece."

Chapter 14

At 5:30 a.m. his eyelids snapped open. It was gray and chill beyond the kitchen window. For a moment he wished it was just another day, get up, out to the park, suck in the cool October air and listen to his sneakers crackling over the fallen yellow leaves. He tried to close his eyes. He rolled over on his stomach and buried his face in the pillow. A bird somewhere, lonely and lost, called for its friends. He turned over on his back. The green plaster over the kitchen sink had finally cracked loose, leaving a powdery-white hole as big as a fist. He wondered why he hadn't noticed it in four months.

After a while the apartment began to stir—first Aunt Pearl, turning heavily in bed for the last few minutes of sleep, then the girls, drowsily untangling their arms and legs. An automobile horn blared downstairs. Garbage can covers clanged. A policeman, bored and tired, dragged his nightstick along the bars of an iron fence. A skinny shaft of sunlight came through the window.

"You sick, Alfred?"

"Feel fine, Aunt Pearl."

"Ain't you gonna run this morning?"

"Not this morning."

"Oh?"

She washed and dressed and woke up the girls. They began wandering between the front room and the bathroom, their eyes half-shut, bumping into each other. Such nice little girls, he thought, warmth spreading through his stomach. See that they get some real cute dresses one of these days.

"You gonna stay in bed all day?"

"For a while."

"You be late for work."

"I'm off today."

"How come?"

"Just like that."

"You ready for breakfast?"

"Just some tea."

"I suppose you want your tea in bed."

"No, I'll get up for it."

"What's going on, Alfred?"

"Nothing."

She let two pots clatter to the floor. Alfred's head jerked up. "Just wanna be sure you're alive," she said.

He put his hands under his head and watched them eat breakfast, smiling as the girls kept peeking at him over their cereal bowls.

"Is Alfred sick?" asked Charlene.

"Alfred has retired," said Aunt Pearl.

"Is Alfred gonna stay in bed all the time?" asked Sandra.

"Why don't you ask Alfred?"

"Today," he said, slowly, "Alfred Brooks is resting himself for his big opportunity for advancement."

"What he say?" asked Paula.

"He don't know himself," said Aunt Pearl. She dropped a tea bag into a cup and poured hot water over it. She placed the cup on the table.

"You been doing so good at the store. They didn't fire you?"

"They did not."

"You didn't hurt yourself with all them exercises?"

"I did not."

She shrugged. "Guess you just a lazy boy."

"Don't you have any more questions?"

She pressed her lips together to stop a smile. "Us busy people don't have time for quiz shows in the morning."

They cleared the table and put on their coats. Aunt Pearl leaned over the bed. "You got a secret?"

"I do."

"Okay." She smiled down at him. "I hope it's something good. Tell me later?"

"Tonight."

"Fine." She touched his forehead. "Don't let your tea get cold."

He got out of bed very slowly, stretched, and took the tea cup into the front room. He turned on the television set, and sprawled out on the couch. He watched two cartoon programs and part of an old gangster movie. He was still sipping at the tea, watching an exercise program for women, when Henry knocked on the door.

"You ain't even dressed yet."

"It's only ten o'clock. We don't have to meet Mr. Donatelli till twelve."

"Yeah, I know. But still."

"C'mon, Henry, I'll make you some tea. Relax you."

He did not begin to feel it himself until they were on the street. His stomach tightened. His lips moved mechanically to smile back at people he knew. They stopped in front of Epsteins' and waved at Lou through the plate-glass window. The old man left the register and came out.

"You feel good?"

"Fine."

"You look good. Get a good night's sleep?"

"Yeah."

"Okay, I don't want you should stand around on the street. I'll see you tonight."

"Tonight?"

"Why not?" said Lou, squeezing Alfred's biceps.

Donatelli was waiting for them at the gym. The room, empty of fighters, seemed huge.

"You have your card?"

"Right here." Alfred opened his wallet and pulled out the amateur card with a postage-stamp photograph.

"Let Henry hold it."

They followed Donatelli downstairs, stopping at the second-floor dentist's office.

"I have a patient now, you better eat without me, Vito," said Dr. Corey. He handed Henry a small box. "I made Alfred a second mouthpiece in case he swallows the first."

"That's not funny, Arthur," said Donatelli.

"So I'm not a comedian." He winked at Alfred. "Don't let these two make you nervous."

Donatelli led them to a small luncheonette around the corner. He ordered sandwiches for himself and Henry, two soft-boiled eggs, toast, and tea with honey for Alfred. The counterman brought the food to their booth.

"You're gettin' to be a stranger, Vito. How's the Streeter kid?"

"I don't handle him anymore."

"Too bad. Got any good ones?"

"They're all good ones."

"Yeah, sure." The counterman laughed.

They picked at their food. "Do you feel butterflies in your stomach?" asked Donatelli.

"No. Like a cold spot."

"That's good. Means you're on edge. The tea will help settle your stomach."

"Henry better have some tea, he's got the butterflies."

The thin lips parted. "That's even better."

On the street again, Donatelli hailed a taxi. He gave Henry a key and three dollar bills. "I'll be up in a few hours. Just make sure Alfred rests." He said something to the driver, and the cab lurched into the uptown traffic.

"Where we going?"

"Spoon's place," said Henry. "Be nice and quiet there."

Alfred relaxed into the back seat. "This is all right. What happens when you turn pro? You get a Cadillac and a chauffeur?"

Henry shook his head. "When Jelly had his first fight, he came back from the weigh-in by subway."

"Hm. Is Jelly gonna fight again soon?"

"I don't know. Just between you and me, Mr. Donatelli ain't so high on him anymore."

"But he knocked the guy out in one round."

"Yeah, but Mr. Donatelli says anybody can't control himself with food can't go all the way. He said that to Jelly's face."

"What Jelly say?"

"He just made a joke, you know Jelly. And then he went out and had a whole chicken. Said he wanted to get an appetite for dinner."

Alfred looked out the cab window. A breeze had sprung up, whipping flecks of white on the Hudson River. The cold spot grew.

"Where's Spoon live?"

"Washington Heights."

"That in Manhattan?"

"Yeah."

Across the river, on a hill, the Ferris wheel of an

amusement park stood motionless against a hazy gray sky.

"Henry?"

"Yeah?"

"You know this is the first time I ever rode in a cab."

"When I was a kid, I rode in a lot of cabs."

"How come?"

"My mother used to take me to the clinic in a cab."

"Oh."

"For my leg. I had polio," said Henry.

"Yeah, I know. I been watching you lately, you don't drag your leg so bad anymore."

For the first time Alfred could remember, the grin completely disappeared from Henry's face. He turned away. "Sometimes it gets a little better. Just temporary."

The cab stopped in front of a six-story brick apartment building on a quiet, tree-lined street. Henry paid the driver and limped heavily to the lobby elevator.

There were more books in Spoon's living room than Alfred had ever seen in a home. The walls were covered with book shelves up to the ceiling. Magazines and records were neatly stacked around the room.

"You think he's read all these books?"

"I don't know," mumbled Henry, lowering himself into a soft chair.

"How you feel, man?"

"Me?"

"Yeah. All I got to do is fight tonight. You, the assistant trainer, got to do all the worrying, right?"

Henry brightened a little. "Spoon says he'd never get to read all these books if he lived to be a hundred, but when him and his wife have an argument all they got to do is look it up and see who's right."

"What do they argue about?"

"I was here one time before and she said the first American to get to the North Pole was black, and he said, No, the black guy and the white guy stepped on it the same time."

"I never even heard about that in school. Who was right?"

"I don't know. They were still looking it up when I had to go."

Alfred laughed. "Some argument. One time I was over this guy's house and his folks got to arguing about cigarettes, and first thing you know they were throwing bottles."

"Bottles?"

"Yeah. Whiskey bottles. They didn't hit each other, but they hit this guy and he had to get nine stitches in his head."

"Was that James?" said Henry.

"How'd you know?"

"I heard it around. You see him anymore?"

"No. I tried to call him a few times but his folks don't know where he's at," said Alfred.

"You were real tight."

"Yeah. He used to be my best friend."

"What happened?"

"You know how it is. Get older."

"What do you mean, Alfred?"

"Forget it. You ever go down the clubroom?"

"Don't you know what happened? Thought you did. They were having a party down there, couple of weeks ago, making a lot of noise and somebody called the cops. They busted in there and found marijuana and heroin—"

"Was James there?"

"Yeah. Everybody beat it except Sonny, he's so dumb. And some kid named Justin. They got arrested. My father kicked them out. It's just an extra storeroom now."

"Where they all hang out now?"

"They scattered."

Alfred pretended to study the books. Many of them were worn around the edges, as if they had been handled often.

"What you thinking about?" asked Henry.

"Huh? Nothing much. Let's see what's on TV."

Henry got up. "I'll turn it on. You gotta rest." He snapped it on. A woman was giving a lesson in French. "You want to watch this?"

"Why not? I might have to fight a Frenchman someday."

"You don't have to talk to him, just hit him."

"Yeah." Alfred pointed a finger at Henry. "You better watch it. You might have to talk to his trainer or something."

Spoon came in a little after three-thirty, a briefcase under his arm. "I always found the worst part of fighting was those long afternoons, just waiting and killing time."

"You must of read a lot of books then," said Alfred.

Spoon shook his head. "Wish I had. No, I used to play solitaire. There was one fighter in those days, a pretty good light-heavyweight named Junior Ellis, who used to sing along with country and western records before a bout. He said it got his fighting juices worked up."

"What happened to him?"

"He had a fight with a top contender, an Italian kid, and lost. The next day, in the papers, the contender said he won because he sang along with opera."

They were still chuckling when a plump, sweet-faced young woman came in. She was carrying a briefcase too. Spoon got up and kissed her.

"This is my wife, Betty. You remember Henry Johnson, and this is Alfred Brooks."

"I'm glad you came up." She shook their hands. "You men sit still. I just have to put Alfred's steak on, and I'll be right out." She went into the kitchen.

"This is a nice place," said Alfred. "Thanks for letting us use it."

"We like it here. Betty can walk to school, and I drive to mine in about twenty minutes."

"Did you get your permanent license?" asked Alfred.

"You remembered. Yes, I did. I'm taking some courses at night for my master's degree now."

"You teach school and go to school?" asked Alfred.

"The more you learn the more you want to know. You ought to think about night school for yourself," said Spoon.

"I didn't graduate from high school," said Alfred.

"You can go to high school at night."

"Yeah?"

"Of course. When you're ready, give us a call. Either Betty or I could find out the night school nearest your home. Or you can do it yourself."

Soon, Betty came out in an apron. "It's ready."

The table was set for one. A large steak sizzled on a plate. There was a bowl of salad, two slices of toast, and tea with honey.

"Go ahead, sit down, Alfred. It's for you."

"What about everybody else?"

"We'll eat later," said Spoon, "while you're taking

your nap. If you eat a big meal too close to a fight there isn't time for proper digestion. Makes you sluggish and slow, and one good punch to the belly and—"

"Billy!" said his wife.

"She's not the world's greatest fight fan," said Spoon.

The steak was thick and rare. He felt funny eating alone, and offered Henry a piece. But Henry just shook his head, and watched him eat, and once told him to chew more carefully. The Witherspoons chattered about school, and about some boy in Betty's class who suddenly quit doing his homework. When Betty called his mother into school, she found out there was trouble at home. Alfred was surprised that a teacher could care so much about some kid not doing his homework.

"You certainly took care of that piece of meat," said Spoon.

"Are you still hungry, Alfred?"

"No, thank you, Mrs. Witherspoon. That was real fine. Thanks a lot."

Spoon stood up. "We'll take a little walk now, give your body a chance to work on that food."

Alfred, Henry, and Spoon strolled around the neighborhood. Men and women were coming home from work in the early twilight. Most of the men were wearing suits and ties.

"A lot of white people live up here," said Alfred.

"This is a fairly well integrated neighborhood," said Spoon.

"You have any white friends?" asked Alfred.

"A few. Some teachers, some college friends, and a boxer with whom I used to train." Spoon laughed. "Once I found out that white boys bled the same color I did I figured I'd let them move into my neighborhood any time."

By the time they returned, Betty had drawn the bedroom drapes and turned down the spread of the double bed.

"Take off your shoes and loosen your belt," Spoon said. "Try to sleep. If you can."

The room was dark, and the murmur of voices outside the door was too low to make out words. The cold spot returned and grew, an ice ball resting in his stomach. He tried not to think about the fight. He took the cab ride again, and thought about Henry, nervous all day and watching over him like a . . . a trainer.

Dishes clattered, and someone said, "Shhh." It sounded like Donatelli. Everybody's been so nice, he thought. I wonder what they'll say if I lose?

The lights snapped on. Henry was beside the bed. "Okay, Alfred, let's go."

Betty shook his hand at the door and wished him luck, and then they were moving quickly, down the elevator, into the darkening street. Donatelli had firm fingers on his arm. They slid into the back of Spoon's car.

"Do you know who I'm going to fight?"

"No. In these one-night amateur shows, the club in charge matches up the fighters at the last minute."

"What if there aren't any other lightweights?"

"That's always a possibility," said Donatelli.

Dr. Corey and Bud were waiting outside the gym. They climbed into the front, Bud carrying his black satchel, an overnight bag, and a large cardboard box.

"What's that?" asked Alfred.

"A third mouthpiece," said Dr. Corey, "in case you swallow the other two."

"Arthur!"

"What's the matter with you, Vito? Laughter is the

best medicine."

"Nobody's sick," snapped Donatelli.

Alfred felt the tenseness in Donatelli's arm, pressed against his own, and the ice ball grew larger and colder. There was little traffic on the streets and over the bridge. The ride ended too quickly, in front of a large, shabby building.

"I'll park the car and meet you afterwards," said Spoon. "Good luck, Alfred."

Donatelli showed tickets to a sleepy old man at the door, and led them through a dark corridor into a large, bare room filled with older men, half-naked boys, and cigar smoke. A gray-haired man came over.

"Good to see you, Vito. This your boy?"

"Right. Alfred Brooks."

"Brooks, Alfred." He made a mark on a clipboard. "Strip down to socks and shorts, Alfred."

The boys in the room eyed each other. The older men called to Bud and Dr. Corey, who waved or shouted back, but Donatelli kept his fingers digging into Alfred's arm.

A doctor came over. He thumped Alfred's chest and back, and placed the cool round end of a stethoscope over his heart.

"Your boy's alive, Vito."

"Yeah, yeah," snapped Donatelli, his voice edgy.

The doctor winked and shone a flashlight into Alfred's eyes, ears, and down his throat. "Have you had any recent injuries, illnesses, dizzy spells, diarrhea—"

"Would I bring him here?" said Donatelli.

"Take it easy, Vito," whispered Bud.

"On the scales," said the doctor. "Brooks. Thirty-four and three-quarters."

The gray-haired man marked his clipboard. "Brooks, black trunks."

Alfred turned to Donatelli.

"Don't worry, Alfred, we brought both black and white." He handed a ticket to Dr. Corey. "You're sitting next to Billy."

"You don't want me in the corner?"

"Henry's working the corner tonight."

LOCAL #143
AMATEUR BOXING
SEE THE CHAMPS OF TOMORROW
TONIGHT
8:30
LONG ISLAND CITY
UNION HALL

Dr. Corey grabbed Alfred's hand. "There's an old saying in—"

"Later, Arthur."

Dr. Corey shrugged, and grabbed Henry's hand. "Good luck."

They hurried outside, past a door marked WHITE TRUNKS AND SECONDS ONLY. Bud led them into a room marked BLACK TRUNKS AND SECONDS ONLY. Half a dozen boys sat and stretched out on wooden benches, surrounded by whispering men. More came in as Alfred pulled on the athletic supporter, protective cup, and black trunks Bud handed to him out of the overnight bag. Henry knelt and laced his white boxing shoes.

"Hands," said Bud, opening his black satchel. He took out two long strips of white cloth and a roll of adhesive tape. Bud and Donatelli each wrapped and taped a hand. Alfred studied a printed poster on the wall.

"Close your eyes," said Henry, opening the large cardboard box.

Something soft and nubby slid over his shoulders. "Open."

It was a snow-white terry-cloth robe.

"Show him the back," said Bud.

Smiling, Henry pulled the robe off and turned it around. Written across the back, in red block letters, was ALFRED BROOKS, NEW YORK.

"Hey, man, you look like you just got hit in the face," said Henry.

"Well . . . I . . . I don't . . . I—"

"You got a lot of sweat in your eyes," said Bud, all gums. He took a sponge from his satchel and patted Alfred's eyes.

"Thanks, I mean . . . I hope—"

"You will," said Donatelli gruffly. "Bud, Henry, let's get the blood circulating, it's chilly in here."

They were massaging his legs and arms when the gray-haired man came in waving his clipboard.

"You go on third, Vito."

"Against who?"

"Kid named Rivera."

"How old is he, what's he weigh, how many—"

"You want to fight or not?"

"Now look, I don't want some—"

"After all these years, Vito, you think I'm going to pull a ringer on you?"

"Easy, man," said Bud. "You know it's nothing personal. We'll take it."

"Sorry," said Donatelli.

"Sure," said the gray-haired man. "I understand." He looked around the room. "Hubbard. Elston Hubbard?"

A powerfully built welterweight with a Marine Corps emblem tattooed in blue on one massive bronze forearm jumped lightly to his feet. "Right here."

"You're on, boy. Jackson, Sam Jackson? You're next." The gray-haired man turned and left.

Hubbard swaggered across the room, two older men trailing him. He turned at the door. "See you cats in a minute," he said, flashing a mouthful of gold teeth.

"That's confidence," said Bud out loud. The fighters and handlers in the room laughed nervously. A tall heavyweight, a little soft around the middle, stood up and began to shadowbox.

"Hands," said Donatelli. He slipped on the gloves, one at a time. Alfred's knees began to quiver.

"How you feel?" whispered Henry.

"Just fine."

The door opened, and the roar of the crowd flooded the room. "Jackson?"

The heavyweight shuffled out with his seconds.

"Stand up," said Donatelli. "Knee bends, that's it, go on down, bounce up, that's the way."

The door opened again, and Hubbard swaggered back in. "Took me one minute, twenty seconds. I'm out of shape."

"Jab," said Donatelli, holding up a hand, palm out. "That's it. Good snap. Let's go."

The ice ball began to melt, trickling freezing water into his legs, stiffening the joints. Donatelli's fingers dug into one arm and Bud's into the other. The crowd noises grew louder as they walked down the corridor and into the back of a square, low-ceilinged meeting hall.

"Ain't Madison Square Garden," said Bud.

"Tonight it is," said Donatelli.

Jackson and another heavyweight were flailing each other in a lumpy, crooked ring in the middle of the hall. Naked bulbs washed the canvas with harsh yellow light. The rest of the hall was in darkness.

Alfred couldn't tell how many people sat in the uneven rows of metal folding chairs.

"C'mon, ya bums," someone shouted. The heavyweights pushed and butted each other clumsily. The referee pulled them apart, and ducked as a long right arm looped over his head. Jackson fell down, and stayed down. He just didn't want to get back up, Alfred thought.

"We're on," said Bud. They started down the aisle, Donatelli and Bud pushing him along with their shoulders. He could hear Henry breathing hard behind them, hurrying to keep up. They waited at the ring steps as Jackson stumbled down, his eyes half-closed, and then they went up, into the pool of hot and blinding light. Bud spread the ropes and Donatelli shoved him through. Rivera was already there, his face blotted out by the lights. He was shorter than Alfred, but very wide and muscular. His legs looked like telephone poles.

"Stick and run, stick and run," whispered Donatelli in his ear, but Alfred was listening to the ring announcer, "In white trunks, from the Bronx, weighing one hundred thirty-six pounds, Joe Rivera. In black trunks, from Harlem, New York, weighing one hundred thirty-four and three-quarters pounds, Alfred Brooks."

The soft, warm terry cloth slipped off his shoulders and Bud's dry stick-fingers were stabbing into his back muscles. "Stick and run, don't slug with him, stick and run, jab and move." Henry shoved the mouthpiece in.

Hands pushed him into the center of the ring and the referee was saying, ". . . three rounds of two minutes each . . . you know the amateur rules . . . break clean . . . shake, boys, and come out fighting."

The ice ball exploded, spraying his entire body

with freezing, paralyzing streams of water, weighing down his arms, deadening his legs, squeezing his heart.

"Stick and run, don't . . ."

The bell rang. He moved numbly forward on stiff legs. Rivera's beady black eyes stared at him over a bent nose.

"Move, Alfred, for . . ."

He walked right into it, a ton of concrete that slammed into his mouth. His arms flew up, and he staggered backwards on his heels. The ropes burned into his back.

The ice ball was gone.

His legs felt like steel springs and his arms were whips. He bounced off the ropes, flicking the jab ahead of him, pop-pop, into Rivera's face, pop-pop, reddening the bent nose. He moved in with a short right, and Rivera walloped him on the side of the head.

"Stick and run, stick and run," screamed Donatelli.

Alfred danced back, sucking in quick, sharp breaths. Rivera was standing in the middle of the ring, his feet flat on the lumpy canvas, planted like a tree. Alfred circled around him, and Rivera turned, slowly and awkwardly, to keep facing him. Rivera wasn't going to move, he was just going to stand there. I'm going to have to go in and get him, thought Alfred.

"Stick, stick, stick and run," screamed Donatelli, but his voice was lost in a rising chorus of boos.

"Get in there and fight, Brooks," someone yelled, high-pitched and nasty, "Off ya bicycle, go and fight."

His body was slick with sweat as he circled Rivera, watching the telephone-pole legs shuffle and turn the squat body. He darted in, pop-pop, and jumped back. Rivera's clumsy left hook missed his head by a foot.

"That's it, Alfred," screamed Donatelli, "just like that, in and out, in and out."

"Fight, ya coward, go in and fight."

"Stick, stick and run."

"Yellow belly, stand and fight."

He darted in again, pop-pop, stand and fight, yellow belly, pop-pop, off your bicycle.

"Move out, Alfred, move . . ."

Pop-pop and he slipped Rivera's slow jab, pop-pop, and he drove in a right cross, stand and fight, and he never saw the punch that slammed into his mouth, snapping back his head. The lights dazzled his eyes, and then a truck crashed into his belly, and a baseball bat blasted the side of his head. He looked up, and the referee was standing over him, wagging a finger, ". . . two . . . three . . ."

The bell rang.

He got up and turned around twice before he saw Bud frantically waving him to their corner. He dropped like a sack on the stool. It seemed like hours before his tongue pushed out the mouthpiece, and then six hands were moving over him, thick, square hands pulling on the elastic waistband of his trunks, "Deep breath, Alfred, deep breath," stick hands stabbing into the muscles of his neck and back, and slim hands tilting the water bottle to his mouth. He gagged on the water and tried to spit it into the bucket in one long stream, but it just gushed out of his mouth over Henry's shoes.

Dimly, he heard the ten-second warning buzzer.

"Stick and run, Alfred," Donatelli whispered into his ear, "don't listen to that crowd, no one's hitting them."

The bell rang.

Rivera was already out there, planted and ready, stick and run, Alfred, stick and run. He darted in, pop-pop, danced back, in and out, in and out, jab and duck, hit and move, circle left, pop-pop, circle right, pop-pop, and he could feel Rivera's blow-torch breaths, hot and heavy against his chest.

"Stand and fight, yellow belly."

Don't listen to the crowd, no one's hitting them, pop-pop, in and out, jab and run away, circle left, and Rivera's eyes were bloodshot and swollen, his thick arms were sagging. Jab and run, dodge, forget the combinations, one punch at a time, two jabs, hit and run, stick and move, don't get too close too long.

"Ahhhhh, go join the track team, Brooks."

The bell rang.

"Smart boxing, Alfred," said Donatelli in his ear, "keep it up, just like that."

"But the—"

"Don't talk, just listen."

The water arched neatly into the bucket. Henry shoved in the mouthpiece. "You won this round, Alfred, it's one each now. Stick and run, stick and run."

The bell rang.

The crowd started whistling, piercing whistles that upset his concentration. Rivera was plodding after him now on slow and heavy feet, pop-pop, stay one step ahead of him, jab and jump away, jab and hook and duck under the swinging arm.

"Run home, ya bum."

In and out, one punch at a time, two jabs, and Rivera was grunting, uh . . . uh, as he tried to find Alfred in the dazzling light and the flying sweat. Pop-pop, hit and run.

"Back to the jungle, ya coward."

The boos flooded the ring and the catcalls burned

his ears and the whistles sliced into his brain. Pop-pop, into Rivera's gasping face. A crumpled paper soda cup landed at his foot, and then another.

"Get in there and fight, black boy."

The buzzer sounded, ten seconds to go, pop-pop, get in there and fight, black boy, pop-pop, you slave, and he drove in, pop-pop, hook, Rivera's eyes were wild, pop-pop and right cross.

"Stick and run, Alfred, don't slug . . ."

Jab-jab hook, right . . . left . . . Rivera tried to bring his arms up . . . jab-jab.

The bell rang, and Rivera slammed a short right uppercut into Alfred's groin.

"The winner, by majority decision, Alfred Brooks."

He barely heard it. His legs were soft rubber and a fire was raging in the lower part of his belly. They carried him back to the dressing room, and stretched him out on the table. Bud held a small bottle under his nose, and the fumes clawed up into his brain, and cleared his head.

"I'm sorry, Brooks." Rivera was standing over him. "I didn't mean to—"

"Forget it, kid," snapped Donatelli. "Any time a fighter gets hit, anywhere, it's his fault."

The circle of faces grew. Spoon, Lou Epstein, Dr. Corey, Henry, Bud, the gray-haired man, the doctor. Fingers probed.

"Be sore for a day or two, but he's all right."

"You can't listen to the crowd," Donatelli was saying, far, far away, "they just want to see blood and pain."

"Leave the boy alone, Vito."

"But he won, Mr. Donatelli," said Henry. "Alfred won."

"That's not enough."

Chapter 15

Aunt Pearl jumped up. "Your face, Alfred, it's all . . . you're limping."

"Looks worse than it is," he said.

"Here, sit down. You want something to eat?"

"Just some milk."

She poured a glass of milk and set it on the table in front of him. She sat down and watched him drink it.

"Want some more?"

"No, thanks."

"You want some aspirin or—"

"I took some already. Doctor gave it to me."

"I'll get your bed ready."

He played with the glass. "Thought you'd have a million questions."

"So you could tell me about the old stone fence off Lenox? A big dog jumped up, right, honey?"

The split in his lip opened again when he smiled. "Yeah."

"I had to find out you was having a boxing fight from Mr. Epstein."

"Thought you might try and stop me."

"You gettin' to be a man, Alfred. I stop you from one thing, you'll do something else."

"You said you didn't like my boxing."

"I still don't. Seems an awful shame, two men got nothing against each other go in and try and beat each other's head."

"I don't know about nothing else."

"Before the summer you didn't know about boxing neither."

"I guess I'll have some more milk."

She leaned over his shoulder and filled his glass. "When I was seventeen, Alfred . . . don't look at me like that, I was seventeen, too . . . a man came by the house. He was from the Apollo Theater. Said he heard me singing in the church choir. Wanted to sign me up for a stage show. No star part, you understand, I'd be in a chorus. Wear a fancy dress. They'd teach me some dance steps."

She walked around the table, holding the milk container with two hands. "Was we ever excited, me and Dorothy and Ernestine, your momma. Couldn't sign a contract because I was underage, and my momma, your grandma, wouldn't sign for me. She said that stage shows were sinful. Be shameful, one of her daughters struttin' around, showin' off. I'd end up no good."

She sat down, her fingers tightening on the container. "How I talked with her, and I cried, and Dorothy and Ernestine, they begged her, too. The more we begged the harder she set her face. Sinful. Shameful. No good."

"You never told me 'bout that."

"No secret. You just always been so closed into yourself, Alfred."

"What happened?"

"Nothing. The man went away. I met your Uncle John, and we went together a long time before my momma would give her blessing. She said he didn't have enough money in the bank. How that man worked. Night and day he worked. We got married, and he got sick soon after Charlene came along. He never did get to see the twins. Passed on a month before they came."

Her hands tightened and twisted on the container, and milk spurted out onto her lap. Alfred came around the table and put his hands on Aunt Pearl's shoulders.

"He woulda been real pleased with them. Nice girls," he said softly.

She was sobbing. "I don't say I woulda been a star or anything. I don't know what I'm saying."

"But you would of liked to try," said Alfred.

"Yes."

He held her shoulders until they stopped heaving.

"Thanks, Alfred. You're a comfort." She wiped her eyes and looked up into his. "I didn't even ask if you won your fight."

"I won it."

She reached up and stroked his face. "And it didn't even taste sweet, the winning, did it, honey?"

"No."

"You gonna quit this thing now?"

"No."

Chapter 16

Griffin was light and fast, his gloves were a red blur tapping away at Alfred's face, easy and steady as rain on a roof, pitter-pat, pitter-pat. Alfred's eyes began to swell and his nose was clogged with dried blood. Donatelli and Henry and Bud were screaming, "Rush him, press, press," but every time he fired out his jab Griffin brushed it aside. By the end of the first round, his face felt as if it had been stung by a hundred bees.

"Attack, attack, two hands," said Donatelli in his ear, and Bud slapped an ice bag against his face. Henry kneaded the muscles of his back. "Go after him, Alfred."

He tried to explain into the ice bag about the red blur and Griffin's speed, but the bell rang. It started again, pitter-pat, pitter-pat, and somebody in the crowd was laughing. He swung wildly, a foot over Griffin's head, and the red blur was back, tapping away at his chin, his eyes, his mouth, his nose. He tried to remember his combinations, left, left, cross, hook, but Griffin's skinny arms knocked his punches away, and then the blur again, pitter-pat, pitter-pat, until he was sure that Griffin had three, maybe five hands at work, all needles and pins stabbing at the bee bites.

The bell rang.

"This is it," said Henry, tilting the water bottle. "Go for the KO, only chance to win, knock his head off."

Pitter-pat, pitter-pat, not quite so fast now, there were only two red gloves, and sometimes he could see them before they tapped against his face. Griffin was breathing hard. He's tired, Alfred thought, tired from hitting me so much. One red glove grazed his ear, the first time Griffin missed all night.

"Rush him, rush him," they screamed from the corner. Somewhere Alfred found a little extra strength, he reached all the way down for it, and the next time the red glove missed he threw his weight behind a short right uppercut.

Griffin stopped cold, a pink blotch on his chest. Alfred swung the hook, everything behind the hook. It slammed into Griffin's jaw. *Thunk*. Pain shot up Alfred's wrist and exploded in his shoulder. Griffin went down and flopped over like a rag doll.

Griffin twitched once, then lay very still on the canvas.

". . . nine . . . ten . . . winner by knockout . . ."

Bud and Donatelli were holding his arms, and Henry was hugging him, but he felt alone and sick. He swallowed back the bitter taste, broke free and ran across the ring.

"Where you goin'?" asked the referee, blocking him.

"Want to see him."

"Later, next bout's coming right in."

"Now," said Alfred, dodging around the referee. Griffin was being pulled to his feet.

"You okay?"

"Huh?"

"I'm sorry I hit you so—"

"Forget it, kid," said one of Griffin's handlers. "Lucky punch."

"Come on, Alfred." Donatelli's fingers were on his arm, pulling him back across the ring. Alfred kept looking over his shoulder as they slapped Griffin awake and helped him down the ring steps.

All the way up the aisle, people stood up and shook their fists and tugged at his robe and cheered. He kept his eyes straight ahead, and his mouth tightly closed. He was afraid he might throw up.

"Let's look at those eyes," said Donatelli, pushing him down on a dressing-room bench.

"Just swollen," said Bud, pressing the ice bag against them. "No damage."

"Beautiful hook," said Henry. "Was that ever a beautiful hook."

"He just lay there—" said Alfred.

"That's part of it," said Donatelli.

"—like a dead man."

"It's happened, Alfred."

Bud took the ice bag away, and looked at Donatelli. They stared at each other for a long time before Bud shook his head, and Donatelli shrugged.

The sound of the hook against Griffin's jaw, the dull, meaty *thunk*, echoed in his mind all the way home in Spoon's car. He heard it in the kitchen, trying to sleep, trying not to see the rag doll flop endlessly to the canvas. He didn't sleep. He left the apartment early, before Aunt Pearl woke up. He didn't want to talk about it over breakfast. He walked through the park, careful to avoid the two policemen. But there was no way to avoid Lou Epstein when he finally went to work.

"Two wins in a row, Alfred."

"Yeah."

"You don't look so good. You want the day off?"

"No, I'm all right."

There were only a few customers that morning. It was hard to concentrate. His fingers were stiff on the cash register keys, and every time he looked up,

Griffin was flopping off a shelf of canned goods. *Thunk*. Lucky punch, beautiful hook. Pitter-pat. NO SALE. Pop-pop-pop, and there was Rivera, and the crowd was screaming, get in there and fight, black boy, coward. Twice, he rang up wrong totals and had to call Jake over to unlock the cash register and correct the receipt roll. All the hate was out in the crowd, he thought, screaming for blood, for a knockout, and the crowd didn't really care who flopped over like a rag doll, Griffin, Rivera, Brooks, anybody.

"Go on, Alfred, take the rest of the day off."

"I'm all right, Mr. Epstein."

"Argue I don't, Alfred. You're fired until tomorrow morning, eight-thirty."

He felt a little better on the street. A brisk November wind tugged at his jacket, and he pulled his cap down over his forehead. It was nearly noon, but the sun was neither warm nor bright. The few people on the street were moving quickly. Across the street, in front of a school gate, two heavily dressed figures were handing out leaflets. One of them waved.

"Brooksy, hey Brooksy. Over here."

He shoved his hands into his jacket pockets and strolled over. Harold was smiling, his eyes were friendly behind his horn-rimmed glasses. Lynn seemed very small and slim, bundled into a tweed coat.

"Hi, Alfred," she said. "We were just talking about you."

"How's that?"

She handed him a leaflet. "Harold was saying how much he'd like to get you involved in our new recreation program."

"That's right," said Harold. "The kids would

really look up to a boxer."

"Only had two fights."

"That doesn't matter. At least you've done something."

"Don't have much time now."

"Think about it anyway," said Lynn. A bell rang inside the school.

"I will," said Alfred, but Harold and Lynn had already turned and begun handing their leaflets to the children streaming out into the street.

He walked on, surrounded by skipping, laughing children. He thought of Rick, the white college boy he and James had liked so much. Alfred half-closed his eyes, okay you little kids, gonna do some push-ups and trunk-twisters, then James here is gonna tell you some funny stories. But James was trembling in the clubroom corner, ripping open his heroin bag, and the crowd was screaming for him to kill Rivera, and Griffin was flopping over like a rag doll. It was too early to go up to the gym, and he didn't feel like watching afternoon television. He dropped Lynn's leaflet into a trash barrel, and headed toward 125th Street and a warm movie.

Chapter 17

Uncle Wilson waved his drumstick. "Two in a row, now that's progress, real progress."

"When's your next fight?" asked Jeff.

"In a week," said Alfred. "And another one a week before Christmas."

"You don't tell me nothing anymore," said Aunt Pearl.

"You worry so much," said Alfred.

"Now, she's got every right to worry," said Aunt Dorothy. "Every day I read in the papers about—"

"Can't hold the boy back," said Wilson. "Top fighter can make contacts with big people, get opportunities."

The room was warm with the nine of them around the table and heat still rising from the turkey, the sweet potatoes, the small mountains of stuffing and green beans. Alfred felt good. Best Thanksgiving ever, he thought, everybody so easy and pleasant, even Wilson. And Jeff was all right, none of those slick, smart-meat college ways he had expected. Lightly he punched Jeff's arm.

"You oughta come up the gym, make a light-heavy out of you."

"I tried it, we had a boxing club in college—"

"You been boxing?" Wilson's drumstick came down in a mound of cranberry sauce. "Get your brains scrambled, waste all that—"

"Wilson." Dorothy pointed at the cranberry stains on his white shirt. The four girls giggled through stuffed mouths, and Pearl raised her napkin to cover a smile.

"I didn't last very long," said Jeff.

"Be glad to show you a few things," said Alfred.

"You forget about that," said Wilson, getting up. He stamped into the kitchen.

"I'd like to be able to handle myself better," said Jeff.

"For Africa?" asked Alfred.

"For anything."

"I hear you talking about Africa?" Wilson came back into the dining room, dabbing at his shirt with a damp towel. "You got accepted and didn't tell me?"

"I haven't sent in the application."

"You better get on with it, boy. Even with your qualifications you can't wait till the last minute."

"I'm not sure I want to go."

"Fine with me," said Dorothy. "I read how they got some tribes running loose over there and—"

"Thought you had your mind set," said Wilson.

"I've been thinking," said Jeff. "All I really want to do was see Africa. Now if I really want to do something positive, I can do it right here in this country."

"Didn't bring you up to be no street worker," said Wilson. "You got the chance to go on out and—"

"Okay. Let's say I go to Africa. Then what?"

"Get a job with a big corporation that—"

"That hires one Negro a year to look good and—"

"Don't you shout at me, Jeff. I know what's best for—"

"Now *you're* shouting, Wilson," said Dorothy.

"That boy just doesn't understand about—"

"Maybe you don't understand," said Jeff.

"Can we go upstairs?" asked Diane.

"Please, please," said the twins.

"Go on," said Dorothy. The girls jumped off their

chairs and clattered away. "You men go on inside and behave. No more shouting. Pearl and I gonna clean up the table. We'll call you back for dessert."

Wilson wandered away after his pipe, and Alfred and Jeff went into the front room. They sprawled out on the couch. Jeff wasn't quite so big as Alfred had remembered. Looks a little like Spoon without the broken nose, he thought.

"Are you going to turn professional?" said Jeff.

"Don't know."

"Do you really like to box?"

"Well—"

"I don't mean to be personal."

"You're my cousin. If you can't be personal—" Alfred shrugged.

"I suppose you wouldn't be doing it if you didn't like it."

"I like it all right, especially the running and the workouts. I like the guys at the gym. But sometimes in the ring, I'm not so sure."

Wilson came into the front room, puffing out clouds of pipe smoke. "How you doing at the store, Alfred?"

"Fine. They're real nice to me."

"Might be thinking about the supermarkets, more money, good benefits, chance for advancement."

"I'm not sure I want to work in a store all my life."

"People always gonna need food, Alfred," said Wilson, pointing his pipe stem. "Can't go wrong working in food."

"Sounds like Jelly Belly," said Alfred.

"Jelly Belly?" asked Jeff.

"Friend of mine at the gym. His real name is Horace Marshall Davenport, Junior, but he's so fat everybody just calls him Jelly Belly. Told me once he'd work at Epsteins' for free if he could eat on the job."

Jeff laughed, but Wilson shook his head. "That's the kind of foolishness gets you nowhere, you got to show them you—"

"Come on in," called Dorothy.

There was ice cream and cake and milk and coffee on the table. Wilson sat down and watched his pipe go out. "Always got to be planning for the future, thinking ahead. Wake up one morning and you find the world passed you by." He looked straight at Jeff. "Right, Alfred?"

Alfred leaned back in his chair. "I've been thinking. I'm gonna continue my education."

"Remembered what I said about trade schools?"

"Finish up high school at night," said Alfred.

"You didn't tell me about that," said Aunt Pearl. "When you decide that?"

"Some time now. Spoon says, more you know, more you want to know."

"Spoon?" asked Jeff.

"Alfred's schoolteacher friend," said Aunt Pearl.

They finished their dessert quietly, and watched Wilson clean and refill his pipe. He lit it and puffed out two quick clouds of smoke. He shook his head. "Sometimes I'm not sure I understand this new generation."

"They got to find their own way," said Aunt Pearl. "Same as we did."

"Times are really changing," said Wilson.

"Men like you started the changing," said Dorothy. "Now it's their turn."

"Couldn't do it without you, Dad," said Jeff.

"Maybe so," said Wilson, leaning back. The smoke clouds rose, slowly and evenly.

Aunt Pearl looked at her watch. "We better go. I have to work tomorrow."

"I'll drive you home," said Jeff.

"That's real nice, but—"

"No, I'd like to, Aunt Pearl. It would give me a chance to talk with Alfred some more."

By the time they dragged the girls from upstairs, and thanked each other for the third time, it was past eleven o'clock. Aunt Pearl, Charlene, and the twins piled into the back of Jeff's old Ford, and fell asleep almost as soon as the car started moving.

"Were you serious about finishing high school?"

"Not until I said it tonight. I'm going to try."

"You've changed a lot," said Jeff.

"What way?"

Jeff stared out the windshield at tiny flakes of snow caught, swirling, in the glare of the headlights. "Well, you always seemed so . . . so negative."

"What do you mean?"

"You sort of seemed to, if you don't mind my saying so, seemed to just drift along."

"Yeah. Sweet old Uncle Alfred."

"Sorry, Alfred, I didn't hear what you said."

"I guess I had no ideas about anything, what I wanted to do, anything like that. Didn't seem like any reason to stay in school. And I wasn't doing good. But Spoon says—"

"The teacher?"

"Right. He used to box. He said if you can concentrate on learning to box, you can concentrate on learning anything."

"That makes sense."

"You were talking before about doing things in this country instead of Africa. Like what?"

"For one thing, a lot of groups are trying to organize self-help programs in the black communities. Parents' groups, tenants' groups. . . ."

"Recreation centers for young kids?"

"Very important. White people have always run those centers and they don't always understand the problems. Black children need to look up to black adults."

"They're working on that around our neighborhood."

"You'd be a natural for something like that," said Jeff. "You have all that athletic background."

"You really think so?"

"I'm sure of it."

Aunt Pearl stirred, and leaned forward. "Better turn here, Jeff."

He squinted through the frosting windshield, and guided the car smoothly to the curb. "Here we are."

Aunt Pearl and the girls kissed him, and sleepily climbed out. Jeff shook Alfred's hand.

"I'll be back for Christmas. See you then?"

"Sure. Maybe you'll come up the gym."

"I'd like that."

"Take it easy, Jeff."

The car pulled away, and Alfred pushed the twins toward the stoop. They whimpered in the cold, and began to wake up.

"You two really got on tonight," said Aunt Pearl. "I never saw you talk so much, Alfred."

They started up the stoop. A shuddering old man crouched alongside the stairs, behind a garbage pail. Poor old wino, thought Alfred. He opened the front door. The huddled figure moved, and Alfred suddenly felt sick.

"I'll be right up, Aunt Pearl. I dropped something."

"You'll catch cold, Alfred," she said. The girls started whining, and she herded them inside.

Alfred moved carefully down the snow-slick stoop, and around the side. The lowered head came up.

"I been waiting on you, Alfred."

"I nearly didn't know you, James. You look so bad."

"You gotta help me."

"Come on upstairs with me. I'll get you some—"

"No." The sunken eyes were very bright and feverish. James shivered inside a torn overcoat. "Loan me some money."

"Hot food, James, come on." He grabbed at the overcoat, but James pulled away.

"I need money."

"For a fix? That won't do you no good."

"I'm gonna quit, Alfred, but I need one more, just one more."

"And after that? Come on, James, come on up."

"Money."

Alfred fumbled in his wallet. He had six dollar bills. A clawlike hand snatched them.

"James, wait, please. I'll—"

But James was weaving down the street, almost running. Alfred watched him until he disappeared around the corner. I should of dragged him up, he thought. What's gonna happen to him now?

Chapter 18

Barnes wasn't as strong as Rivera or as quick as Griffin, but he was rough and dirty in the clinches. He held Alfred's arms, stepped on his toes, pounded his kidneys. Donatelli screamed, "Break loose, push away," but Alfred's arms were heavy, his legs glued to the canvas.

"What's wrong with you?" snarled Donatelli. Water gurgled into his mouth as Alfred tried to think of an answer. Six hands moved over his body, the ice bag slapped against the back of his neck.

The crowd was booing, but he didn't care. If you want to see blood, he thought, go punch each other. He felt tired, his brain felt tired, his eyes were watering. He threw out his jab mechanically, just stiff enough to keep Barnes away. Once, Barnes tried to duck the jab, and stumbled, his unprotected face bobbing up six inches from Alfred's right fist. "Nail 'im," screamed Henry, but Griffin's twitching body flashed in Alfred's mind, and he never threw the punch.

Barnes clinched and started pounding on his kidneys again. Alfred looked over Barnes' shoulder at the clock on the far wall. Another thirty seconds. The referee pulled them apart, and Alfred kept Barnes away with the jab until the final bell rang.

". . . decision of the judges . . . a draw. . . ."

The crowd booed him back to the dressing room. Donatelli and Bud and Henry and Spoon and Dr. Corey shifted from foot to foot as he dressed. He avoided their eyes. The ride back to Manhattan was silent. Spoon stopped at the gym first, to let Donatelli out.

"I want you to come up, Alfred," said Donatelli.

They walked slowly up the sagging stairs. Donatelli unlocked the gym door, and went into the darkness to find the light string. When Alfred went in, Donatelli was standing under the single naked bulb, his face smooth and hard. Like the first night, Alfred thought. Donatelli put his arm across Alfred's shoulders. His voice was soft, almost gentle.

"It's time, Alfred."

"You want me to quit?"

"To retire," said Donatelli.

"What about the next fight?"

"I'll cancel it."

"Why?"

"You don't have the killer instinct, Alfred, the coldness to beat a man into the ground when you sense his weakness. I'm not sure I'd want you to have it."

"Not all boxers have it."

"Some are so good they don't need it. You're not that good."

"I could try."

"You did, Alfred." Donatelli raised one bushy white eyebrow. "You don't really like to fight, do you?"

Alfred lowered his head.

Donatelli took his arm away and walked over to the plate-glass window. "I'll never forget how you came up those dark steps. Alone. At night. Scared. You conquered your fear. You worked hard. You almost quit once, and then you came back and worked harder."

"Mr. Donatelli?"

"Yes?"

"Remember what you said that night . . . about being a . . . a contender?"

"Yes."

"You weren't just talking about boxing."

"You understood that."

"And what you said about quitting before you really tried."

"You've tried. I know you've tried."

"The next fight, I—"

"No. You've had three fights now and never lost. They won't match you with the Riveras and the Griffins and the Barneses anymore. They'll put you in with someone who could hurt you, really hurt you."

"Be like not finishing."

"That's not true. You've learned to work hard, to concentrate. To climb." He left the window and came back to Alfred's side. "I'd like you to keep training, keep running, spar with the new boys coming up. Like Spoon does. But no more fights."

"You got to let me finish."

"There are other things you want to do now, aren't there, Alfred?"

"Yes."

"You'll do them. I know you will," said Donatelli.

"Got to finish."

"But why?"

"So I can know, too."

Chapter 19

"You are nervous," said Henry.

"Always nervous before a fight. Means I'm on edge. Ready."

"Sure. And you always read books upside down."

Alfred pushed the book into the shelf, and dropped back into one of Spoon's overstuffed living-room chairs. "What time is it?"

"Five minutes after it was last time you asked."

"What was that?"

"It's two-thirty," said Henry.

"Exactly two-thirty?"

"Two minutes before two-thirty, all right?"

"Why don't you say so?"

Henry shrugged himself deeper into the couch.

"Man, you are something. Want some tea?"

"No."

"Play cards?"

"No."

"Want to see some TV?"

"I don't care."

"Maybe we'll get another French lesson," said Henry.

"Yeah. Maybe you'll train a Frenchman someday."

Henry brushed some invisible lint off his knee. "I'm sorry, Alfred."

"What are you sorry about?"

"Gonna be your last fight."

"Yeah."

"Maybe if you—"

"No chance. Mr. Donatelli said even if I win big, it's all over," said Alfred.

"You gonna keep coming up the gym?" asked Henry.

"I guess so."

"Alfred?"

"Yeah?"

"Why you so nervous?"

"Told you. Always nervous before a fight."

"But it don't matter."

"Matters to me."

"Alfred?"

"Yeah."

"Tell you something?"

"What's that?"

"Remember that time you said I wasn't limping so bad anymore?"

"Do I? You looked like I kicked you in the belly."

"You were right. I don't limp so bad anymore."

"Why's that?"

Henry began brushing both knees at once. "Don't think about my leg so much. Since I started working for Mr. Donatelli and helping train you, it just don't bother me so much. Sound weird to you?"

"Don't sound weird at all. You gonna keep training boxers?"

"Yeah. Mr. Donatelli says he wants me to start working with new kids coming up soon as—" Henry closed his mouth.

"Soon as you don't have to spend so much time with me. Right?"

Henry nodded.

"That's okay." Alfred stretched out his legs, and worked his hands into his pockets. "Only got to use my robe three times. Keep it clean tonight and you can take my name off, use it for somebody else."

"That's your robe."

"I won't need—"

"Your robe. I bought it for you."

Alfred sat up. "You bought it?"

"Yeah."

"I always thought it was Mr. Donatelli. You bought it?"

Henry smiled, a nice easy smile, nothing like the old plastered-on grin. "You were my first fighter. You got me my start."

"You had the job."

"Just to clean up around the gym. You were the first fighter I helped train. The first time I got to work a corner was for you. I'll never forget you, Alfred."

They sank back into their seats, and stared at specks of dust climbing and circling in a weak shaft of winter sunlight. Henry was quiet, barely moving. Alfred concentrated on the little cold spot growing in his stomach. He wondered if he would ever feel it again, for anything.

"Are you guys hypnotized?" Spoon burst into the apartment, peeling off his overcoat and throwing down his briefcase in one movement. "Did I have a day and a half today. Boy pulled a knife on me in the school yard."

"You knock him out?" asked Henry.

"No. Poor kid had enough beatings in his life. I spent the afternoon trying to explain to him why that knife isn't going to do him any good. It was like going ten rounds." Spoon loosened his tie. "He told me he's scared to walk around without a knife, so I suggested he go down to the gym and look up either of you two guys. His name is Herbert Davis."

"I'll watch for him," said Henry.

"Good." Spoon opened his briefcase, and pulled out some sheets of mimeographed paper. "I got that night-school reading list for you, Alfred."

"Thanks." Alfred stood up, and took it. "Lot of books."

"You can get a start before the semester begins," said Spoon. "We have most of the books here. If you come up next week, when Betty and I are off for Christmas, we can go over them together."

Betty bustled in a few minutes later, and started chattering with Spoon about her day at school. Alfred folded the list carefully and slipped it into a pocket. He closed his eyes and tuned out the chatter. He concentrated on the cold spot again. Got to remember the feeling, he thought, it's like an old friend you're never going to meet again. New friends coming up, new things to do, but never that cold spot growing in your stomach, telling you you're on edge, ready for something big, streams of chilly water running all over your body, and exploding when you have to get in there and fight.

"Steak's ready."

He ate slowly, tasting each bite, a little sorry to swallow because then there was one bite less of the last steak. They took their walk slowly too. Henry and Spoon said nothing, letting Alfred think his thoughts. The last walk.

Spoon led him into the darkened bedroom, and closed the door behind them. "I talked to that doctor at the narcotics clinic, Alfred. He can find a place for your friend. But he says that you'd have to do most of the work. Even after an addict takes a cure, he needs a great deal of encouragement to stay off drugs."

Alfred pulled off his shoes, and lay down. "I can't find him. He cut out of the neighborhood again."

"Let me know when he turns up." Spoon left.

Alfred stared up at the ceiling, at the white streaks

that flashed overhead when cars passed on the street below. The cold spot became an ice ball, just like the first time he had lain on this bed, staring at this ceiling, listening to the murmur of voices outside, the soft clink of glasses and dishes. Long time ago, that first fight. A million years.

The light snapped on. Henry looked sad. "Let's go, Alfred."

At the door, Donatelli's pale blue eyes searched Alfred's face, but the thin lips never moved. They filed slowly out of the apartment. Alfred turned at the door and took Betty's outstretched hand.

"Thanks for all the steaks. They were real fine. Goodbye."

She patted his hand. "When you come next week I'll cook something different. And we'll eat together for a change. Good luck."

They all found things to stare at in the elevator, and they each looked out a different window as Spoon drove downtown. Even Dr. Corey had nothing to say when he and Bud climbed into the car in front of the gym.

He tried to remember every little thing so he could store it away for later, the ticket man nodding them into the building as if it was just another fight night, the other boxers looking him up and down in the dressing room as if he'd be an opponent some day, the extra care Henry and Bud took winding the cloth strips around his hands.

"How's your stomach?" asked Donatelli.

"Cold."

"Good. I'd be worried if it wasn't."

The door opened. "Brooks? You go on in the second bout."

"Against who?" asked Donatelli.

"Kid named Hubbard, only one in your class."

"Elston Hubbard?"

The man looked at his clipboard. "That's the kid."

"Forget it." Donatelli stood up. "You can untape Alfred's hands, Henry."

The man stepped into the room. "You don't want the fight?"

"Not against Hubbard."

"Wait now." Alfred pulled his hands away from Henry. "I want the fight."

"No, you don't," said Donatelli. "Hubbard's twenty-two, twenty-three, at least seven pounds—"

"I want the fight."

"You'll get hurt," said Donatelli.

The man tapped his clipboard. "Well?"

"Just one minute, mister," said Alfred. "Look, Mr. Donatelli, remember how you said the only way you'd ever know is if I got hurt, really hurt in the ring?"

"But it doesn't matter now."

"Does to me."

"You don't have to prove anything to me, Alfred."

"To me I do."

A red flush crept up Donatelli's close-shaven cheeks. "You'll have to get yourself another manager, Alfred, one that doesn't mind a little blood."

"You're my manager, and you're gonna be in my corner."

"What makes you so sure?"

"You're not gonna walk out on me now. You took me this far, you told me all that stuff about being a contender, and you ain't quitting on me now, not when I got a chance to find out, my last chance—"

"It's not your last chance."

"In boxing it is."

The man rapped his clipboard against the door. "You can argue all night, but I got a program to—"

"All right," snarled Donatelli. "Put us on second."

"Hands," said Bud.

They slipped on the gloves and laced them tight.

"Jab," said Donatelli, holding up his palm.

The ice ball was gone, completely gone, and Alfred had trouble finding his voice. It finally came out high and thin. "You understand, Mr. Donatelli, I got to."

"I understand. Jab."

He swung his arms, and loosened up his legs. The door opened again. The crowd was booing outside.

"Brooks?"

"We're ready," said Donatelli.

They went down the aisle three abreast, Donatelli and Henry moving him along with their shoulders, Bud right behind with the towels and the bucket, up the ring steps and through the ropes. Elston Hubbard was already in the ring, flexing his forearm muscles so the Marine Corps emblem jumped on the smooth bronze skin. The ring lights glinted off his gold teeth when he grinned at Alfred and then out at the crowd. Hubbard held up his right arm, and the crowd cheered.

Just before the bell, Alfred thought he heard Donatelli whisper, "Be careful, Alfred," but it was lost in the roar of the crowd and Henry's scream, "Look out."

Hubbard's face was on top of him and something slammed against the side of his head. The canvas floor came up and smashed into his nose.

". . . three . . . four . . . five . . ."

A gray shirt and a black bow tie hovered above him, and a forefinger waved in his face. ". . . six . . . seven . . ."

He got up.

The referee grabbed his gloves and wiped them off on his gray shirt. "You okay, boy?"

"Yeah."

"What's your name?"

"Alfred Brooks."

"Okay, go on and fight."

Hubbard rushed out of the corner, swinging his left like a meat hook. Alfred sidestepped and snapped a left jab into the charging forehead, then another, pop-pop, but the head came on and crashed into his mouth, hurling him against the ropes. Concrete gloves hammered into his stomach, his sides. The ropes burned across his back. Hubbard's hard body forced him backwards, Hubbard's shoe tips slashed at his ankles, knotty shoulders bumped up into his chin, and the bullet head ground into his eyes. Hubbard was pummeling his ribs now, and Alfred worked his left arm free and began banging at the side of the bullet head, again and again and again, until Hubbard straightened up. Alfred lunged forward on his left foot, and spun away from the ropes. He leaped into the center of the ring.

Far, far away, someone was yelling, "Stick, stick, stick and run . . ."

Up on the balls of your feet, chin in, here he comes, left, left, pop-pop, circle, left, shift, cross. An iron pipe rammed into the pit of his stomach, turning his legs to rubber. *Whomp.* He never saw the punch, but he heard it thud against his ear and then the distant plop, like a stone splashing into the pool at the bottom of a sewer hole. He staggered, dizzy, a sudden coolness deep in his ear.

". . . four . . . five . . . six . . ."

He got up.

"Where are you, boy?"

"Parkway Gardens. Brooklyn."

"Okay."

Left . . . left . . . hook . . . cross, once he thought

Hubbard's head jerked back, but then the iron pipes were ramming into his stomach, one after another. Drop your elbows. *Whomp*. He went backwards on his heels, into the ropes. Here he comes, left . . .

The bell rang.

His tongue filled his mouth. Henry had to pull out the mouthpiece, and the cold sponge turned hot on his face. Whatever Donatelli was whispering into his ear fell right to the bottom of the sewer hole, plop. Black stick fingers smeared yellow paste on his eyebrows, stinging him awake.

The bell rang.

Up on the balls of your feet, chin in, stick and run, stick it out, jab and move. Why don't they turn out those lights, blinding me, here he comes, stick, stick, uh . . . Hubbard drove him into the corner, the wooden post slammed into the back of his neck. Hubbard was marching in place, like a soldier, marine, pounding, pounding, iron pipes, sledgehammers, belly, chest, throat, chin. Keep doing it, man, keep doing it. If you stop now I'll just go down, melt down like butter and leak right off the canvas. *Thunk*.

". . . six . . . seven . . . eight . . ."

He got up.

"Had enough, boy?"

"Fine, I'm fine."

"Who you fighting?"

"Elston Hubbard."

"What round is this?"

"Round two."

"Okay."

Stick, stick, cross, hook, pop-pop, he never stops, pop-pop. They clinched in the center of the ring. Hubbard raked his laces across Alfred's rope burns, and stepped on his toes, and rubbed his jaw against

Alfred's, the stubble of his beard like sandpaper on Alfred's skin. He threw Alfred away, across the ring, and rushed after him, swinging. Iron pipes again, sledgehammers, meat hooks.

The bell rang.

"You want him to continue?" asked the referee.

Donatelli's pale blue eyes were narrow.

Henry's voice, shrill and loud. "Gotta let him, Mr. Donatelli, gotta."

"Let him fight," said Donatelli.

The bell rang.

The crowd was roaring deep in its gut, ocean waves that lapped at the ring, that drowned all pain and all feeling, drowned all sound but the drumming of leather against flesh. Everything was wet and sticky. Everything was sweat and blood. There were three Hubbards now, all of them hazy, jab at the middle one, hook the middle one. They stood toe to toe in the center of the ring, whacking, slugging, thumping back and forth, flinging sweat, elbows, fists, knees, jab the middle one, hook the middle one. *Thunk.* Alfred felt his mouthpiece fly out, hook the middle one, pop-pop, iron pipes, sledgehammers, meat hooks, go ahead, throw everything you got, you gonna have to, gonna stand here all day and all night and take what you got and give it right back, gonna hang in forever, gonna climb, man, gonna keep climbing, you can't knock me out, nobody ever gonna knock me out, you wanna stop me you better kill me.

The bell rang, but neither of them heard it, grunting, straining, slugging, and then everyone was in the ring pulling them apart, grabbing their gloves.

". . . by unanimous decision . . . Elston Hubbard."

The referee held up Hubbard's right arm, and his manager held up the left, but Hubbard broke loose and ran across the ring, throwing his arms around Alfred. They hugged each other, crying because it was over, and Hubbard gasped, "You tough, baby."

All the way up the aisle, people were reaching out to touch Alfred's robe. "Great fight, kid . . . beautiful . . . real heart, Brooks . . ." The dressing room was jammed, Lou Epstein clutching his gloves, "Like the old days, like the . . ." Jose and Angel screaming, Spoon reaching for him, Jelly and Pete Krakover, Denny slapping his back.

"Let him breathe," bellowed Bud, pushing them all out and slamming the door shut. Henry began to unlace his gloves.

Three Donatellis peered down into his face, then two. His eyes finally focused. The thin lips were parted. Donatelli was smiling.

"Now you know, Alfred. Now you know, too."

Chapter 20

Aunt Pearl's hands were clenched and her eyes were wide when he bounded into the apartment.

"Shoulda called and told you I'd be so late." He smiled through cracked lips. "We all went out, Mr. Donatelli, Spoon, everybody. Jelly's got this new job at a fancy restaurant, number-three vegetable man, six round meals a day, he says—who wants square meals—and we all—"

"Alfred, the—"

"Don't mind all this tape on my face." He kissed her damp forehead, and peeled off his coat. "Looks worse than it is, I feel—"

"—police were here."

"Police?" He let his coat and cap fall to the kitchen floor. "What for?"

"They're after James."

"What's he done?"

"He broke into Epsteins' tonight, right through the front window. They saw him, but he got away."

"Why they come here?"

"They were very nice and all. They knew from last time you and James was friends."

"Right through the front window?"

"Why'd he do a fool thing like that, Alfred?"

He shrugged. "Well, I hope he gets away."

"I don't think he's gonna."

"Why not?"

"The police said he cut himself real bad getting out again. Blood all over. They said he can't get too far."

"James," whispered Alfred.

"Police said they think he's a . . . Alfred, where you . . . ALFRED!"

He took the steps two, three at a time, stumbling twice, and he hit the icy stoop off-balance, tumbling into the street, but he was up and running hard, into the bitter night wind that lashed at his thin sweater and blew wet flakes of snow into his face, running out the stitch that chewed at his side, running into his second wind, feeling the cold spot grow and explode in his stomach. He didn't slow down until he reached the park.

The park lay white and silent, the new-fallen snow glistening under a full moon. The snow deadened his careful footsteps, over the smaller rocks, over the low thicket of leafless bushes. He dropped to his knees in the shadow of the huge rock, and elbowed his way through the stunted trees. At the mouth of the cave he heard heavy breathing.

"James," he whispered.

The breathing stopped.

"It's me. Alfred."

"What you want?"

"Come to help you," said Alfred.

"Just go 'way."

He moved in closer, his knees quivering as the snow seeped through his trousers.

"Go 'way."

"My cave, too, James. Remember?"

He crawled in. A wooden match flared, and he saw James, crouched like a cat, his eyes wide, sweat bubbling on his face. Before the match burned down into James' fingertips, Alfred saw the dark, widening stain on his torn coat sleeve, and the blood running off his hand.

"You're cut bad."

"That's my business."

"Need to go to a hospital. I'll take you."

"Leave me 'lone."

"If you don't bleed to death, you could get infected."

"Too bad."

"This ain't the movies, James. You could lose your arm."

The breathing began to slow down, grow shallower.

"James?"

"It hurts."

"Let me wrap it up."

James lit another match. Alfred ripped off the torn coat sleeve and tied his handkerchief around the cut. The handkerchief turned red, but the flow of blood slowed down.

"All that tape on your face."

"Had a fight tonight," said Alfred.

"You win?"

"Sort of."

"You a fighter. Always so meek and quiet."

"Let's go."

"You got any money, Alfred?"

"For a fix?"

"You said you was gonna help me."

"That's not gonna help, just mess you up more."

"Just one more."

"You said that last time."

"What do you know?" James began to sob, his shoulders heaving. Dirt and pebbles spilled off the ceiling of the cave.

"You can beat the junk, man, I'm gonna help you beat it," said Alfred.

"I ain't hooked. I can stop any time. Just one more."

"Look at you, like a garbage rat. You hooked all

right. But you and me can beat it."

"It's no use."

"Remember Mosely of the Jungle and Bad Brooks?"

"No."

"Sure you do. Remember how we used to hide here? Remember the night my momma died and you stayed with me, told me you were gonna stick with me? Sure needed you that night."

"I got chills."

"You and me, James. Gonna stick with you. I got friends, Henry and Bud and Mr. Donatelli, help get you in shape after you beat the junk. Spoon, you'd like him, got more books than anybody."

"It ain't no use." The voice was soft and weak.

"I'm gonna go to night school. You come too. Gonna work in a recreation center for little kids, you come help me. You was always so comical. Get you a job."

"Grocery boy," said James.

"For start. Nothing's promised you, man, but you ain't gonna know nothing till you try. Maybe get to build things like you always wanted."

"Whitey ain't gonna—"

"Dare him to stop you. Dare anybody if you and me partners again."

"I'm too sick. I need a fix."

"Gonna take you to the hospital now."

"They'll call the police."

"Can't do nothing about that."

"I'm on probation, they'll send me away this time."

"Maybe, maybe not. Mr. Epstein'll help if I ask him. Even if they send you away, won't be forever. I'll be around. Gonna get you clean, man, and gonna keep you clean."

"Alfred?"

"I'm right here."

"Why you wanna do all this?"

"Because I know I can, James. And you're my partner. Ready?"

There was no answer. Alfred's fingers moved up James' arm. The blood was flowing again. "That's the way you want it, James. I'm gonna go. Good luck."

He began edging backwards out of the cave, scraping his feet as noisily as he could. "So long, James."

"Alfred?"

"Yeah?"

"Okay."

Alfred scrabbled back in, reaching, feeling James' outstretched arms around his neck. Slowly, he pulled James out of the cave into the biting wind.

"Easy, man, you be all right." He lifted James to his feet and half-carried him through the stunted trees. James moaned.

"Hang in there, James. Can you walk?"

"Try." He leaned heavily on Alfred. "Weak as a baby. Lost all that blood."

"Don't worry about that, James, I got plenty of blood for you." Carefully, Alfred guided him over the rocks and the bushes and the new snow, toward the lights of the avenue.

Related Readings

CONTENTS

The Seventh Round

by James Merrill

Imagine competing in an arena or a stadium and hearing the crowd cheer on your opponent. The speaker of this poem describes such a situation. What do you think Alfred Brooks might have said about the speaker's response?

Give it to him!
To you, they mean.
As always (mezzanine
Gone dazzling dim,

5   A crown at stake)
Before you stands
The giver with clenched hands.
Drop your own. Take.

Fury

by T. Ernesto Bethancourt

*When his life was heading nowhere,
Alfred Brooks stumbled into Donatelli's
gym. Under Donatelli's direction, Alfred
began to train to be a boxer. In this story,
Randy, like Alfred, learns the discipline of
boxing. How would you compare Alfred
and Randy?*

It was after midnight when Harlow Fuller heard his dog barking in the front yard. He was in his bedroom, in the neat, five-room brick house he'd owned for years. He put down the magazine he'd been reading and went cautiously to the front door. A baseball bat stood in the corner behind the door. South Jamaica was a bit safer than ghetto Brooklyn, but here, where people owned their homes, the burglary rate was higher.

Harlow peeked through the drawn curtains on his barred windows. He saw a large young man standing at his front gate. From behind the gate, Emile, Harlow's huge Doberman, was barking wildly. Harlow went to the front door and opened it a crack.

"Who's out there? What do you want at this hour?" he called.

"Uncle Harlow? It's me—Randy Fuller."

"What are you doing out here in Jamaica?"

"I can explain, if you let me in."

Harlow stepped outside. "Emile!" he said softly. "Place!" The dog stopped barking immediately and trotted over to Harlow's side, where he sat down and looked up at his master. "Good boy," Harlow said, rubbing the dog's ears.

"It's okay, Randy," Harlow called to the boy at the gate. "You can come in. Emile won't bother you now." He turned and went inside. Randy entered the yard and followed his uncle into the house.

Once inside, Harlow said, "Well, let's have a look at you, boy. Last time I saw you, you were . . . ten years old, I think. At your daddy's funeral. You've sure grown."

There was no denying Randy's size. He stood two inches over six feet. When Randy took off his light windbreaker, under which he wore a T-shirt, Harlow noticed the young man's barrel chest and thickly muscled arms. He whistled softly.

"Seems we got us a heavyweight in the family," Harlow observed. "I can't believe how much you look like your daddy. He could have been a fine boxer, you know. I offered to train him, but your mamma was dead against it.

"So your daddy stayed on, driving a truck. And what happened? He gets hit by a drunk with no insurance. Some safe job.

"I said that to your mamma at the funeral. Bert would have been safer in the ring. She hasn't talked to me since. I'm not welcome at your mamma's house. That's why I'm so surprised that you showed up here. And at this hour. What's going on, Randy?"

Randy shifted in the chair, facing Harlow. "I'm in bad trouble, Uncle Harlow. Police are looking for me."

"What did you do, boy?"

"Nothing, really. I was just there when something happened."

Harlow threw back his head and laughed loudly. "Half the cons in the joint say the same thing, Randy.

Suppose you back up a bit and tell me just what went down."

"I was helping out a pal," Randy said. "His name is . . . *was* Eddie Sanger. Some dude owed Eddie some money. Eddie asked me to come with him to collect it."

"Hold on," Harlow said. "What did this 'dude' owe Eddie the money for?"

Randy avoided his uncle's eyes. "That's what Eddie does for a living—he loans out money."

"And this was the first time you ever went with Eddie to collect?"

"Uh . . . no. I done it before."

"And Eddie paid you, right?"

"Uh-huh."

"Then let's get things straight, boy. You were strong-arming for a loan shark when this 'something' happened."

"I wouldn't put it that way," Randy said.

Harlow smiled. "I can think of a half dozen judges and DAs who *would*. But go on with your story."

"When me and Eddie found the guy, I had to run him down. He was taking off on us. I knocked him down on the sidewalk, right off Ralph Avenue and Jefferson Street.

"All of a sudden, the dude pulls out a piece and starts shooting. I didn't know Eddie had a gun, too. Before I know it, there's bullets flying all over. I got out of there, fast. I took in a movie over on Broadway." He reached over to his jacket and took out a ticket stub.

"Figuring that if anyone came looking for you, you'd say you were at the movie all along?" Harlow asked.

Randy nodded. "When I got back to my street, there was talk already. Eddie was dead. The other guy was in the hospital in bad shape. But word on the street was that he's saying Eddie shot at him first. And the cops are looking for me."

"I'm not a bit surprised. But what brought you out here to me, Randy?"

"Well, Mamma always talks about how you were in trouble once. That you did time, upstate. I thought maybe you, knowing about these things, could tell me what to do."

Harlow shook his head. "Francie always had a mouth on her. Did she ever tell you what I was in for?"

"No."

"I was in for being stupid, that's what for. I did six years out of eighteen for manslaughter. I killed a man with these." Harlow held up two knotted fists. "Some fool got wise with my woman one night at a restaurant. He swung at me when I told him to buzz off. I punched him out. But he hit his head on a table when he fell. He died."

"Then it wasn't your fault," Randy said.

"Oh, but it was. I was a pro—a boxer. To the law, my hands were deadly weapons. And it was my fault, too. I could have talked my way out of it. But a hot temper runs in the Fuller family. Your daddy had it too. It could have made him great in the ring. But it's no good if you can't control it outside the ring. That's what happened to me."

"And you did all that time for it."

"Nowhere near what it could have been. After a few years, I got another lawyer and a new trial. When I came out, I was an ex-con. I lost my license to fight. It was hard to stay straight. Then I started in training young fighters that I thought looked good—kids who could be champs. I've done okay. I get respect as a businessman these days. But I still haven't found my champ—that kid who can make it all the way to the top."

"So you never were a real criminal, were you?"

"Sorry to let you down, Randy. I was stupid and made a bad mistake. I paid for it, too. Even one day in a cage would be too much. I did over two thousand days. Most hotheaded kids never know what it's like inside—until it's too late."

Harlow got up from his chair. "Now, what am I going to do with you, kid?" He saw the look on Randy's face. "Don't worry—I ain't going to turn you in. But it's a matter of time before the police start checking out the whole family. They *will* come here, sooner or later."

"If I can stay a few days . . . ," Randy began.

"Are you hungry, kid?" Harlow asked. "Did you eat at all today?"

"Not since breakfast."

"You go on into the kitchen. Help yourself to what's in the freezer. You know how to run a microwave?"

"Yeah."

"Get yourself something, then. I have to go down to the basement and set up a place for you to sleep."

"In the basement?"

"Can't have you up here. I got a finished basement down there, though. I got a door that locks from the outside. If anyone checked, they could see no one's using my other bedroom. I'm gone in the daytime, at my gym on Jamaica Avenue. Emile keeps people away from the place while I'm out."

"He's some kind of dog."

"Ain't he ever? I named him for Emile Griffith. That's what Emile looked like when he was welterweight champ. All muscle, steel wires, and teeth. Now, you get something to eat while I go downstairs."

A half hour later, Randy followed his uncle down the basement stairs. Harlow swung open a door to a large, wood-paneled room. There was a mattress in one corner. A heavy bag hung from a chain in the center of the room, and a light speed bag was in the far corner. On the walls were bright, shiny weights for bodybuilding. Between two paneled doors was a rowing machine. The only light came from a bare bulb that hung from the low ceiling.

"Okay, kid," Harlow said. "It ain't much, but it's going to be your home for a time. You can't keep the light on at night—people could see it through the basement windows." He waved at the barred windows set high in the walls. "Once the sun comes up, you'll have light enough down here."

"But what will I do down here?" Randy protested. "There's no radio, no TV—"

"What do you think you'd have in jail, boy?" snapped Harlow. "You want to do something, hit the speed bag or the heavy bag. There's a pair of workout gloves in that closet and some sweats that should fit you. They're mine. There's a little john behind that other door. I'll bring you a toothbrush and some shaving stuff when I get back from work tomorrow. Now I have to get some sleep."

Harlow closed the door and shut off the light switch alongside it. "But this is like jail!" Randy protested from behind the door.

"You don't know what jail is," Harlow said. "You got your own health club in there, kid. Use it."

He went upstairs, brushed his teeth, and went to bed. As he turned out the light, he heard a slow, regular thumping sound from the basement. He smiled. "Fool kid's hitting that heavy bag in the dark," he thought as he drifted off. "Yeah, no doubt of it. He's got that Fuller hot blood."

Early the next morning, Randy was awakened by a rough hand on his shoulder. Without thinking, he swung hard at its owner. His large fist hit nothing but air. He opened his eyes, for a moment not remembering where he was. He saw his uncle standing over him, smiling.

"You do wake up a bit sudden, don't you, Randy?" Harlow said.

"What time is it?"

"Six o'clock. Time to be up and doing, boy!"

"Leave me alone," Randy grunted, rolling over. "I don't get up at home until noon."

"This ain't home, kid," Harlow said. He grabbed at one corner of the mattress on the floor and tugged mightily. Randy rolled out onto the hard tile. The young man got to his feet with fists at the ready. Harlow laughed.

"Come on, kid. Anytime you're ready."

Randy rushed at the older man, swinging a wild, overhand right. Harlow barely moved. As the force of the blow carried Randy past him, Harlow gave the younger man a hard shove that sent him sprawling onto the floor.

Harlow then threw the mattress over Randy. As the young man got to his hands and knees under the mattress, Harlow placed a well-aimed kick on his padded rear. Even through the mattress, he could hear Randy's grunt of surprise and pain.

"This is no way to treat somebody who's brought you breakfast, Randy," Harlow said to the form on the floor. "Aren't you hungry?"

"*Mmmmph*" came from under the mattress.

"I guess that means yes," the older man said. He walked to the open door and picked up a tray from the bottom step of the stairs. When he returned, Randy was sitting up in the center of the floor.

Harlow set the tray before him.

"What's this?" Randy asked, eyeing the tray.

"High-protein drink, high-fiber cereal, and skim milk. Some complex carbohydrates and a handful of vitamins."

"This is garbage," Randy said. "Ain't you got any Froot Loops?"

"You're something else, boy," Harlow answered. "Here you show up at my house, on the run. I take you in, give you a nice place to stay, and you try to punch me out. Then you complain about the eats. You sure got a short grip on being grateful, boy." He pointed to the tray. "If you're hungry, eat it. If not, I'll be taking it with me, along with the mattress."

"What are you taking that for?" Randy asked. He had secretly intended to go back to sleep once his uncle had left.

"I got it off the bed in my spare room. If anyone came by to look for you, they'd wonder where the mattress was.

"I'm going to be gone for most of the day. When I get back, we'll have dinner."

"But what will I do for lunch?"

"That's why I gave you such a big and healthy breakfast. Eat it, or don't." Harlow grinned widely as Randy began to try the cereal. He was still smiling as he locked the heavy door behind him and tugged the mattress upstairs. As he reached the top step, he heard Randy call out through the door.

"What am I supposed to do in here all day?"

"You could do a couple of things," Harlow called back. "You could think on how you got yourself into this mess. And you could also do your body some good. You may look okay, but you're slow on the punch. The only thing you could hit for sure is the floor."

As Harlow left the house, he could hear thumping coming from the basement. He paused outside to feed Emile before getting into his car. He patted the dog and whispered, "You take care of things around here, Emile. I think we got us a heavyweight, all right."

It was growing dark when Harlow returned to his home. He was greeted by Emile. He reached into his car, took out a large paper sack, and walked into the house. He checked his answering machine, then went downstairs. As he did, he heard the *rat-a-tat* of the speed bag. It didn't last long. But then it began again, after some muffled curses from Randy.

Harlow unlocked the door to find Randy flailing away at the speed bag. "I told you that you had slow hands," Harlow said, setting the paper sack on the floor. "Didn't anyone show you how to use that bag right?"

Randy turned and looked at his uncle sullenly. "Nobody ever showed me nothing. But I had to do something. I'm going crazy down here."

"After only one day? What do you think you'd do in a jail cell?"

"Maybe I'd have somebody to talk to there."

"Maybe you would. But I'll tell you this: In the six years I listened to jail talk and yard talk, I never heard anything worth two cents. And best you get used to being here. It may be a while before you see the outside."

"What are you talking about?"

"That 'dude' you told me about. His name was Arnold Jensen—the homeboys called him Zipper, right?"

"Yeah. How did you know?"

"He's in the papers, Randy. He died last night

from the gunshots. Now the cops really want to talk to you."

Randy sat down on the floor and put his head in his hands. "What am I gonna do?" he moaned. "I told you I didn't have nothing to do with the shooting part."

"I believe you. But the police might not. That's why I bought this today." He reached into the paper sack and took out a long yellow legal pad.

"You're going to write down exactly what happened. Then you're going to sign it. After that, I'll send it to the police."

Randy got to his feet. "Are you crazy? Soon as they get that, they'll be here!"

"Oh, I don't think so," Harlow said. "I'll mail it to one of the kids I used to train. He lives in Detroit. He'll send it from there. With no return address, all the cops will have is a Detroit postmark."

"That's great of you, Uncle Harlow! Now, when can I get out of this room?"

"Hold on! First, the cops won't stop looking until after they get this paper from Detroit, and probably not even then," Harlow looked up at the ceiling. "In fact, they could show up here anytime. The best place for you right now is here in the basement. Now, let's get started on getting your story on paper."

A half hour later, Randy crumpled up another yellow page and threw it across the room. "It's no good!" he complained. "I can't write this out myself."

"Didn't they teach you anything in school? Or didn't you pay attention?"

"Didn't see no need for school," Randy grumbled.

"Okay. I'll write it down and you copy it, word for word. It's got to be in your handwriting. It will give you something to do tomorrow." Harlow pointed to the paper sack. "I got you a razor and shaving cream and a toothbrush. There's some new underwear in there, too. I got extra-large. Is that right?"

"I don't know. Mamma buys all that."

Harlow roared with laughter. "Some tough guy you are. What are you? Eighteen . . . nineteen years old and your mamma still buys your clothes!"

Randy jumped to his feet. "You got no call bagging on me."

Harlow backed off in mock fear. "Oh, please don't hit me, Mr. Tough Guy," he moaned. "Otherwise, I'll have to tell your mamma!"

With a roar of rage, Randy rushed at Harlow. The older man ducked under a roundhouse right hand and stepped lightly to one side. Then he hit Randy in the gut with a blow that caused the younger man to let out his breath in a giant *whoosh!* Randy fell to his hands and knees, gasping for air.

Harlow stood over him. "Not only do you have slow hands, you got a soft belly, boy. Must be all those Froot Loops you eat. I hope I didn't spoil your dinner with that punch. I got you something real healthy tonight."

"Like that breakfast?" asked Randy from the floor.

"Much better. You be nice to me, I'll let you have some extra wheat germ on it. And if you eat it all up, I'll show you how to work that speed bag."

The next morning when Harlow awoke, he heard the speed bag going like a machine gun. "The boy learns fast," he thought. "If he keeps it up, it ain't going to be so easy keeping him down there—Oops! almost forgot!"

Harlow took a book from the shelf alongside his

bed. Then he went downstairs and opened the door. Randy was at the speed bag, his hands moving just as Harlow had shown him the night before. He looked up as Harlow entered. The older man tossed the book to him.

"What's this?" Randy asked.

"When you get all punched out, you could look it over," Harlow said. "It helped me when I was in the joint."

Randy looked at the thin book. Painfully, he formed his lips around the words on the cover. "*Yes . . . I . . . Can . . . R-Read.*"

It was four days later when Harlow came running down the stairs. Randy was working out in silent fury. He barely looked up when Harlow burst into the room.

"Quick, Randy—into the shower stall!" Harlow commanded.

"What for? I ain't finished working out."

"There's a police car just pulled up in front. Do what I say. I'm going to open up this room. Show them the closet, too. With the john door open, I don't think they'll check the shower stall. Pull the curtain closed, though." From the floor above, the doorbell began to ring. "No more time," Harlow whispered. "Be cool, kid."

Harlow quickly locked the door and ran up the stairs. Randy heard voices and the heavy tread of feet above him. He remained inside the shower stall. A few moments later, he heard footsteps coming down the stairs.

"What's in there, Mr. Fuller?" Randy heard a strange voice saying.

"My private workout room. I'll show it to you."

"You don't have to, sir. We have no warrant—"

"No, I insist." The lightbulb went on in the basement room. "No one can say I didn't cooperate with the Police Department."

Randy pressed himself tightly against the wall of the shower stall, hoping it would make him appear smaller. Was Uncle Harlow going crazy? Why was he bringing the cops downstairs?

"What's behind that door?" Randy heard the policeman say.

"A closet," Harlow answered. "I'll show you."

"No need," the cop said. "I've seen enough. Thank you for your help, Mr. Fuller. And if you do see Randy . . ."

"I'll be sure to call you."

The light went out again, and Randy heard the door being locked. He stood inside the stall for the longest time, shaking all over. After what seemed like years, the footsteps overhead stopped and he heard the front door close heavily. Shortly after that, he heard Harlow coming downstairs.

"Okay, Randy," Harlow said softly. "You can come out." Still unsteady, Randy came out into the main room. "That was awful close, Uncle Harlow," he said. "Why'd you bring him down here? I heard him say he didn't have no warrant."

"Use your head. If I told him he couldn't look, he'd have gone to a judge and got the papers. This way, I showed him I have nothing to hide."

"I guess they didn't get that letter from Detroit yet," Randy said.

"Even if they did, they probably wouldn't give up. This is a murder case. That stays on the books forever."

"Then what am I going to do? I can't stay down here for the rest of my life."

"You won't have to. Once things blow over a bit,

we'll get you a good lawyer. In the meantime, you got no choice but this." Harlow looked around at the small room.

"But I can see why you feel boxed in down here. Now that the cops won't be back, maybe we can start you on some roadwork. You can run off some of that anger of yours."

"But where? Won't someone see us?"

"Baisley Park is four blocks from here. We'll run early in the morning while it's still dark."

"I heard about Baisley Park. That's a dangerous place after dark."

Harlow laughed loudly. "You mean you're scared? The reason people stay away from the park is they don't want to run into someone like *you*! You're the one who's on the run from the police.

"Besides, we'll take Emile with us. He needs to run, too. I figure two guys our size and a dog like Emile, no one's going to mess with us."

And so began a regular routine of roadwork and bodybuilding for Randy. Each morning, Harlow would drive to the park and the two men and the dog would run until nearly sunrise.

Harlow noted that it helped Randy's spirits. The young man no longer complained about being cooped up. His body shed fat and gained hard ropes of muscle. Randy continued to work endlessly on the two punching bags and the rowing machine. Often, Harlow would hear Randy continuing to work out in the dark.

What made Harlow feel best was that Randy had finished *Yes, I Can Read*. But at the end of each day, Randy would have the same questions: "When do I get out of here? When are we going to get that lawyer?"

Each time Harlow said, "When I think it's cool,

and no sooner." Randy would grow more restless. Finally, one night in early September, he exploded.

"I don't care what you say!" he shouted at Harlow. "I'm leaving. It's been almost four months. I'll take my chances outside. Anything is better than this!"

"You watch yourself, boy," Harlow said, "or I'll take away your roadwork. How would you like that?"

"How would you like me to walk right over you?" Randy growled.

"You think you're man enough?"

In a dark rage, Randy sprang at him. A looping left hand banged into Harlow's ribs, and like lightning, a stiff right hand to his head followed.

As Randy was about to throw another punch, Harlow dodged, hooked a foot behind the younger man's left ankle, and tripped him. Randy tried to regain his balance, but Harlow stepped in and with three short punches knocked him to the floor.

His head buzzing from the blows, Randy looked up at his uncle. "You cheated!" he cried.

"You bet I did," Harlow answered. "No way I'm going to bust my hands on your hard head. And there's not enough room down here to fight. But if that's what you want, that's what you'll get. Tonight I'll sneak you over to my gym. We'll put on the gloves and settle this right!"

The gym was on the second floor of a run-down building, in the shadow of the el. Harlow opened the double-locked steel door and hit a light switch inside the doorway. "Go through that door behind the ring," he said. "The lockers are in there."

In a few minutes, Harlow had pieced together shoes, shorts, and sixteen-ounce gloves for Randy and himself. "One more thing," he said to the younger man. "Put this on, too." He handed Randy some headgear.

"What do I need that for?" Randy asked.

"We already know you can hit hard," Harlow said. "But we don't know how hard a punch you can take. I don't want to scramble the inside of your head."

The two men climbed into the ring. "We don't have a bell or timekeeper," Harlow said, "so there won't be any rounds. When I say 'go,' you start fighting. When you're ready to quit, just say 'when.' Ready?"

"Yeah, I am."

"Then go!"

As Harlow expected, Randy came on in a rush, swinging wildly. For the first few minutes, all Harlow did was avoid the rushes and tag Randy with a left or right hand as he went past. But after a time, Randy stopped being wild. A cold, hard look came over his face and he began to stalk Harlow.

Seconds later, Randy connected with a straight left hand that rocked his uncle. He held on, then wrestled Randy into the nearest corner.

Once his head cleared, Harlow put together a savage left, then a right to Randy's body. He finished with a stinging left hook that caught Randy square on the headgear. Randy went down.

"Had enough?" Harlow asked, standing over his nephew.

"I'll say when," Randy growled, getting up.

It began again. Was it his imagination, Harlow wondered, or was the kid getting stronger? Over the next ten minutes it took all of Harlow's skills to hit and not get hit. And still the boy came on. He shook off punches that would have taken him out only months before.

For all of Harlow's coaching in the basement, Randy seemed to learn better by doing, in the ring. He connected with a solid right to the middle of Harlow's chest. It felt like a small car had hit him; he was actually pushed back a few steps by the force of the blow. And still Randy came on!

Harlow felt his strength fading—an experience he hadn't known in years. He had always kept himself in superb shape. But this nephew of his didn't seem human. Harlow showered a group of punches on Randy, finishing with a right cross that knocked the younger man to his knees.

Breathing hard, Harlow said, "Had enough yet?"

To his amazement, Randy was getting up again! "I'll say when," he said.

This time, Harlow didn't back off and allow Randy to regain his senses. With all he had left, Harlow hammered his nephew to the canvas. Again, he stood over the young man.

"Enough?" he asked. Randy shook his head and tried to get to his feet! Harlow put a hand on his nephew's headgear and pushed him to the canvas. "Well, *I've* had enough," he said. "You got heart, boy. Seems to beat you, I'd have to kill you. And I'm not ready to do that."

Randy stayed down. Harlow pulled off his gloves and reached a hand out to help him up. To his surprise, a thundering right hand caught him flush on the chin, knocking him onto the seat of his shorts. Randy was on his feet like a cat. He looked down at Harlow.

"I been trying to catch you standing still all night," he said. "Now I did."

"You cheated!" Harlow accused.

"You bet I did," Randy replied. "Same as you did, back at your house. But I got to say you did beat me, fair and square."

Harlow sat up and roared with laughter. He took the hand that Randy extended and got to his feet. As they left the ring, Harlow began talking. "See, you couldn't get at me because of the way I was moving. And you got to stop dropping that left jab after you throw it. I came over that left with my right all three times I dropped you.

"That left jab has got to snap out straight and come back just as fast. You practice and you can double up the jab. That's a real setup for a right hand." He rubbed his rib cage. "And you got some right hand on you, kid. I'm going to get you a mirror for the basement, so you can see what you're doing better."

"The basement again!" Randy moaned. "When do I get out of there? When do we get that lawyer?"

"I'll make you a deal, Randy. When you beat me, you're out of that room."

"You got a deal, Uncle. When's our next fight?"

Harlow groaned in mock pain. "Soon as I get over this one." Both men laughed, then walked together to the locker room.

The next three weeks marked an even greater change in Randy. Harlow had given him a copy of *The Ring Encyclopedia*. Though Randy had shown some interest in easy-to-read stories, this new book was something different.

Randy began asking Harlow to help him sound out words in the book. And it seemed that Randy could remember almost everything he read—so long as it was about boxing.

As always, he went at his workouts in a rage, but it was different now. It was a cold anger. Randy stopped wasting his moves. He paid attention to every detail.

When he and Harlow ran in the park, Randy

would reel off the names, dates, and winners of title fights, going back for years. Sometimes he seemed to know more than Harlow about the subject.

Every time Randy would ask a question about boxing history that Harlow couldn't answer, it pleased the younger man. It was as though he had won something personally over Harlow.

But on the subject of leaving the basement room, Randy was unchanged. It was in early October that he greeted his uncle with: "I'm ready for that rematch. We still have the same deal?"

"Same deal," Harlow answered. "You beat me— we get the lawyer, and you get out of the downstairs."

When they came up the stairs and Harlow simply pushed the door to the gym open, Randy looked at his uncle in surprise. "Did you forget to lock up?" he asked.

"I'd sooner forget my head," Harlow replied. "I called someone to be here. To keep time and count for knockdowns. We're going to go six rounds, boy."

As the two men entered, an attractive woman of about thirty came out of Harlow's office. She was over five feet seven inches, Randy judged, and her well-muscled form was properly shown off by the jeans and light sweater she wore.

"Hey, Danielle," called Harlow. "I got someone I want you to meet." Harlow saw the look of near panic on Randy's face and whispered as Danielle approached. "It's okay. She's cool."

"But she's a woman!" Randy whispered.

"Sure is, isn't she?" Harlow said, grinning. "And she knows her boxing, too. Try some of your questions on her."

"What questions are those?" asked the young woman.

"This is my nephew Randy. I told you about him on the phone. He's some kind of expert on the fight game, Danielle."

Danielle looked Randy over with a cool gaze. "Good-sized kid," she said to Harlow. "How much do you weigh, Randy?"

"Two-ten. But don't you say 'hello' or 'pleased to meet you,' lady?" asked Randy.

"I don't get social with fighters," Danielle answered. "Bad enough I go out with Harlow. But what did you want to ask me?"

Randy was silent for a moment, his mind racing. "Who beat Tommy Burns for the heavyweight title in 1908?"

Danielle laughed. "You joking? Jack Johnson. He held the title from 1908 to 1915."

"Let me ask *you* one. Name the only heavyweight champs who retired undefeated."

"That's easy. Rocky Marciano and Joe Louis."

"Wrong!" crowed the woman. "You forgot about Jim Jeffries. He quit the fight game in 1905."

"I ain't that far back in the book," grumbled Randy. "Besides, I ain't into any of the fights before black men had a chance at the titles."

"I don't know what book you're reading, but you better read it better. There were other black men in boxing before Jack Johnson. Check out the other weight divisions, Randy."

"I told you she knew her stuff," Harlow said. "Now, let's get set for our little rumble, okay? You hit the locker room. I'll be there in a minute. And don't forget your headgear."

When Randy had left, Danielle fixed Harlow with

a hard look. "Are you sure you know what you're doing, Harlow? You told me that kid's been in heavy training for almost six months. And you've been teaching him all you know.

"You got a few pounds on him, that's true. But face it, man, you're forty. If he's got any real stuff, that kid can do you world-class harm."

"Now, that's real caring of you, Danni," Harlow responded, "looking out for an old man. But I didn't say I showed the boy *everything* I know. I still got some stuff he's never seen."

"I'm looking out for the fancy dinner you promised me. And I want both of us in shape to eat it. Now how about you get ready, too?"

In a few minutes, Harlow and Randy were standing in the middle of the ring, with Danni between them. "All right, you two," she said. "I can't be in the ring and work the bell, too. And all I can time rounds with is my watch." She raised her wrist to show a sports watch with a built-in stopwatch.

"When I say 'fight!' you go at it. If you clinch and I say 'break!' you break, and break clean. When I holler 'stop!' you quit, or I'll take points away. I keep score, and whoever I say wins is the winner. You got that?"

Both men nodded. "You're going to be your own seconds. And you won't get to sit down between rounds. I can't be shuffling buckets and stools around. If there's a knockdown, you get to the nearest neutral corner. I won't start counting till you do. Now, go to your corners and don't come out till I say so."

The two men went to opposite corners. Danni raised her hands over her head, then brought them down, smacking her palms together. "Fight!" she cried out.

Randy moved in fast. Harlow began a circling motion, blocking or slipping past Randy's punches. Each time Randy would be about to get set, Harlow would hit him with a quick left, then circle again, always keeping the younger man off-balance.

As he continued the pattern, Randy's punches kept getting closer. Still, the only solid blows struck were by the older man. Ten seconds before Danni cried "Stop!" Randy missed a punch aimed at Harlow's head, and instead caught him on the left shoulder.

Harlow felt like he'd been hit with a hammer. For a second, he lost feeling in his left arm. "I got to slow this kid down," Harlow thought as he stood in his corner, his mouthpiece in his hand.

Almost before he knew it, Danni had called out "Fight!" again, and Randy was closing in. This time Harlow appeared to stand his ground. As the younger man closed, Harlow moved his left shoulder but threw a hard, right-hand lead that caught Randy flush on the button. The younger man was knocked onto the seat of his pants in the center of the ring.

Danni waved Harlow to the far corner and began a count. But by the time she got to four, Randy was on his feet. "Hold on!" Danni cried to Harlow. "Standing eight count here!"

She finished the count and cried "Fight!" Randy moved in again, this time keeping his hands higher. As Harlow began to circle again, Randy kept after him, cutting off the ring and working his uncle toward a corner. It was there that Harlow experienced the roughest few seconds of his entire career.

Randy let loose a series of lightning-fast short blows to Harlow's body. Every time Randy hit him,

Harlow felt the pain. But when Randy shifted his attack "upstairs," Harlow slipped two blows. Bouncing off the ropes, he punched his way out of trouble. As he moved away, he connected with a straight left hand that he felt hit the mark.

For years Harlow had practiced this "going away" punch, made famous by the great Sugar Ray Robinson. He had knocked men cold with it. Now Harlow felt the force of the blow throughout his whole body. But Randy just took the shot, blinked, and moved in—just as Danni called "Stop!"

As Harlow stood in his corner, breathing heavily, Danni approached him, with one eye on her stopwatch. "You okay?" she asked.

"Yeah," Harlow said. "But you didn't do me no favor with that standing eight."

"Don't complain," Danni said. "The way it's going, you might need one yourself. That kid is real good. A little green, but he's good. You take care of yourself, Harlow."

"I'm trying! I'm trying!"

Danni called "Fight!" and it began again. After the harm done in the corner, Harlow wasn't moving well. His ribs hurt, and his punches were slower. Still Randy came on. Harlow landed a three-punch combination that should have knocked the younger man down. It didn't even slow Randy.

Harlow got set to try the right-hand lead that had floored Randy earlier, and suddenly his world exploded in a shower of bright light. When he opened his eyes, he was looking into Danni's. "What? . . ." he said.

"What do you think?" Danni replied. "He tagged you. Before you could throw that right, he put a straight left in your dumb face. You scared me, man. You were really out."

"Where's Randy?"

"I told him to hit the showers. You going to be all right?"

"Yeah . . . I think so. Man, that boy can hit!"

Harlow got to his feet and walked with Danielle to his office, where he sat down heavily at his desk. Danielle took off his gloves, then talked with Harlow for the next few minutes. Finally, cleaned up and wearing street clothes, Randy came into Harlow's office.

"Are you okay, Uncle Harlow?" he asked.

"Fine, boy . . . just fine. I got to admit you beat me."

"Hard not to admit," said Danni, "when they scrape you off the canvas."

"This might not be the time," Randy said, "but how about that lawyer?"

Harlow waved a hand at Danielle. "Go ahead and talk. You're looking at her."

"You're a lawyer?" Randy gasped at Danni.

"One of the best," Harlow said. "She gave me a lot of help in getting your case together."

"Case?"

"Yes, Randy," Danni said. "I've been involved since last June. That's when Harlow told me what had happened with you in Brooklyn."

Randy turned to Harlow. "But you told me . . ."

"It's complicated, Randy," Harlow said. "Why don't you just listen to what Danni has to say?"

"You're in trouble, all right, Randy. But not as big as you think," Danni said. "Yes, you were at the scene of a crime. And your connection to it isn't the cleanest. But you didn't do the crime.

"As to that, both people involved in the double murder—Eddie and Zipper—are dead. I talked to the police and to a judge. Nobody is going to miss either one of them too much. But you saw it all happen, Randy. Did you ever hear of a material witness?"

"No . . ."

"Well, that's what you were. In fact, some of Zipper's friends were looking for you. The police only wanted your statement as to what happened. Zipper's friends were after your head. There were two things the police could have done. One was lock you up to keep you safe."

"In jail?"

"No place safer, except if you were being hidden by a responsible person. In your case, you had a family member—Harlow—who is also an assistant probation officer."

Randy turned to Harlow. "You're a cop!" he accused. "And all that time you had me in that little room, you were lying to me! And you lied about you getting into trouble, I bet!"

"No, Randy. That part's true. But your mamma has the same ideas about ex-cons that lots of people do—that they can't go straight. I went back to school when I got out. Got my degree in social work. Working with the Probation Department, I opened this gym.

"I try to keep kids like you from getting into big trouble by putting them into boxing. It was a way of putting together my talent for athletics and my new career."

Harlow waved at the wall of pictures behind his desk. "All these kids you see were in trouble when I found them. I'm proud of all of them. Some of them went on to be pretty fair fighters. Others have good jobs and are making something of their lives."

"But cops came to your house looking for me. I heard them. You told me to hide."

"I sent for them. After all, I *am* with the Probation

Department, kid. I was afraid you'd run off at first—maybe go back to the neighborhood and get hurt. Yeah, I lied to you. It was to keep you in one piece.

"Besides, I saw early on that you had talent as a fighter—just like your daddy did. And what were you doing with your life, anyway? You were on your way to big trouble."

"That don't matter!" Randy shouted. "It's my life, ain't it? Who gave you the right to play God?"

"Your mamma, for one. Yeah, you're over eighteen, Randy. And I didn't much care for talking with Francie. But once I told her what my new career was, and that I was keeping you safe, she was all for it. Maybe what I did wasn't all that fair, but look at you now.

"When you came to my house, you were big and thought you were tough. But you were soft and couldn't hit the floor if you fell out of bed. I made you into a real athlete. You're even reading now, and getting better every day at it. You've done something with your life these past months. You've made yourself into a person your mamma could be proud of."

Randy's face was a mask of dark rage. He moved toward Harlow. "I ought to . . . ," he began.

Harlow held up a hand. "What are you going to do? Beat up on me? You already did that. Are you going to do something stupid, like I did, outside the ring? Or are you going to put that hot blood of yours to good use? You're what I've been looking for all these years. You could be a champion, Randy."

"And I think I can get charges reduced because you cooperated with the police," Danni added.

"I what?"

"You gave a full statement, in your own handwriting. Your uncle saw to that. Then you stayed with him—a probation officer—until the hearing. That's coming up next month, by the way."

"But that still didn't give him the right to do what he done to me!"

"Keep you in protective custody? That's what a judge called it. Think it over, Randy," Danni said.

"I've already did that. I'm out of here!" Randy left Harlow's office and headed for the door.

"Randy!" Harlow called after him. "It's chilly out there. You don't have anything but summer clothes on. You could get sick."

"It ain't any colder than what you done to me," Randy called back. He slammed the door behind him.

Harlow looked at Danni, then leaned forward over his desk, his head in his hands. "I've lost him, Danni," he said.

"You did your best," Danni said, putting a hand on the big man's shoulder. "Why don't you shower and change? I'll start shutting down here. And you still owe me a dinner. We'll talk over some food, okay?"

Harlow nodded and went off to clean up. When he walked back to his office in street clothes, he couldn't believe his eyes. Randy was sitting in his office, talking with Danielle. The young man looked up as Harlow entered.

"Randy! You came back!" Harlow cried.

"Didn't have subway money," Randy grumbled. "Didn't even have money for a phone call. I been in your jail so long, I forgot about money."

"I gave him some money," Danni said to Harlow. "That's more you owe me."

"Then how come you're still here?" Harlow asked Randy.

"I had to ask you something. You already lied to me so much, I don't know what to believe. But did you mean it when you said I could be a champion?"

"More than anything I've ever said in my life. If you work at it as hard as you have been."

Randy looked hard at Harlow, then asked, "Can I use your phone?"

"Help yourself."

Danni and Harlow stood outside the office door while Randy dialed. Through the partly open door, Harlow could hear Randy's side of the conversation.

"Hello . . . Mamma? Yeah, it's me. . . . I'm just fine. Say listen, Mamma. Would you mind if I stayed with Uncle Harlow a while longer? No . . . I'm not sure how long. I'll send you a letter about it, Mamma. . . . Sure, in my own handwriting. What, do you think I can't? Yeah . . . I love you too, Mamma. Bye."

When Randy came out of the office, he looked at Harlow and Danni and smiled. "What's for dinner, Uncle?" he asked.

from The Story of My Life

by Helen Keller

*In this selection from her autobiography,
Helen Keller describes what her life was
like before and after Anne Sullivan, her
teacher, entered it. As you read, consider
Anne Sullivan's influence on Helen. Then
compare it with Donatelli's influence on
Alfred.*

I was born on June 27, 1880, in Tuscumbia, a little
town of northern Alabama. The beginning of my life
was simple and much like every other little life. I
came, I saw, I conquered, as the first baby in the
family always does.

I am told that while I was still in long dresses I
showed many signs of an eager, self-asserting
disposition. Everything that I saw other people do I
insisted upon imitating. At six months, I could pipe
out "How d'ye," and one day I attracted everyone's
attention by saying "Tea, tea, tea" quite plainly. Even
after my illness I remembered one of the words I had
learned in these early months. It was the word
"water," and I continued to make some sound for
that word after all other speech was lost. I ceased
making the sound "wah-wah" only when I learned
to spell the word.

They tell me I walked the day I was a year old. My
mother had just taken me out of the bathtub and was
holding me in her lap, when I was suddenly attracted

by the flickering shadows of leaves that danced in the sunlight on the smooth floor. I slipped from my mother's lap and almost ran toward them. The impulse gone, I fell down and cried for her to take me up in her arms.

These happy days did not last long. One brief spring, musical with the song of robin and mockingbird, one summer rich in fruit and roses, one autumn of gold and crimson sped by and left their gifts at the feet of an eager, delighted child. Then, in the dreary month of February, came the illness that closed my eyes and ears and plunged me into the unconsciousness of a new-born baby. They called it acute congestion of the stomach and brain. The doctor thought I could not live. Early one morning, however, the fever left me, as suddenly and mysteriously as it had come. There was great rejoicing in the family that morning, but no one, not even the doctor, knew that I should never see nor hear again.

Night

I cannot recall what happened during the first months after my illness. I only know that I sat in my mother's lap or clung to her dress as she went about her household duties. My hands felt every object and observed every motion, and in this way I learned to know many things. Soon I felt the need of some communication with others and began to make crude signs. A shake of the head meant "No" and a nod, "Yes;" a pull meant "Come" and a push, "Go." Was it bread that I wanted? Then I would imitate the acts of cutting the slices and buttering them. If I wanted my mother to make ice cream for dinner, I made the sign for working the freezer and shivered, indicating cold. My mother, moreover, succeeded in making me understand a good deal. I always knew when she wished me to bring her something, and I would run upstairs or anywhere else she indicated. Indeed, I owe to her loving wisdom all that was bright and good in my long night.

I understood a great deal of what was going on about me. At five I learned to fold and put away the clean clothes when they were brought in from the laundry, and I knew my own from the rest. I knew by the way my mother and aunt dressed when they were going out, and I always begged to go with them. I was always sent for when there was company, and when the guests took their leave, I waved my hand to them, I think with a vague remembrance of the meaning of the gesture.

I do not remember when I first realized that I was different from other people; but I knew it before my teacher came to me. I had noticed that my mother and my friends did not use signs as I did when they wanted anything done, but talked with their mouths. Sometimes I stood between two persons who were conversing and touched their lips. I could not understand and was vexed. I moved my lips and gestured frantically without result. This made me so angry at times that I kicked and screamed until I was exhausted.

I think I knew when I was naughty, for I knew that it hurt Ella, my nurse, to kick her, and when my fit of temper was over I had a feeling similar to regret. But I cannot remember any instance in which this feeling prevented me from repeating the naughtiness when I failed to get what I wanted.

Many incidents of those early years are fixed in my memory, isolated, but clear and distinct, making the sense of that silent, aimless, dayless life all the more intense.

One day I happened to spill water on my apron, and I spread it out to dry before the fire which was flickering on the sitting-room hearth. The apron did not dry quickly enough to suit me, so I drew nearer and threw it right over the hot ashes. The fire leaped into life; the flames encircled me so that in a moment my clothes were blazing. I made a terrified noise that brought Viny, my old nurse, to the rescue. Throwing a blanket over me, she almost suffocated me, but she put out the fire. Except for my hands and hair I was not badly burned.

About this time I found out the use of a key. One morning I locked my mother up in the pantry, where she was obliged to remain three hours, as the servants were in a detached part of the house. She kept pounding on the door, while I sat outside on the porch steps and laughed with glee as I felt the jar of the pounding. This most naughty prank of mine convinced my parents that I must be taught as soon as possible.

The Search for Help

Meanwhile the desire to express myself grew. The few signs I used became less and less adequate, and my failures to make myself understood were invariably followed by outbursts of passion. I felt as if invisible hands were holding me, and I made frantic efforts to free myself. I struggled—not that struggling helped matters, but the spirit of resistance was strong within me; I generally broke down in tears and physical exhaustion. If my mother happened to be near, I crept into her arms, too miserable even to remember the cause of the tempest. After awhile, the need of some means of communication became so urgent that these outbursts occurred daily, sometimes hourly.

My parents were deeply grieved and perplexed. We lived a long way from any school for the blind or the deaf, and it seemed unlikely that anyone would come to such an out-of-the-way place as Tuscumbia to teach a child who was both deaf and blind. Indeed, my friends and relatives sometimes doubted whether I could be taught. My mother's only ray of hope came from Dickens's "American Notes." She had read his account of Laura Bridgman, and she remembered vaguely that Laura was deaf and blind, yet had been educated. But she also remembered with a hopeless pang that Dr. Howe, who had discovered the way to teach the deaf and blind, had been dead many years. His methods had probably died with him; and, if they had not, how was a little girl in a far-off town in Alabama to receive the benefit of them?

When I was about six years old, my father heard of an eminent eye doctor in Baltimore, who had been successful in many cases that had seemed hopeless. My parents at once determined to take me to Baltimore to see if anything could be done for my eyes.

When we arrived in Baltimore, Dr. Chisholm received us kindly, but he could do nothing. He said, however, that I could be educated. He advised my father to consult Dr. Alexander Graham Bell, of Washington, who would be able to give him information about schools and teachers of deaf or blind children. Acting on the doctor's advice, we went immediately to Washington to see Dr. Bell, my father with a sad heart and many misgivings, I wholly unconscious of his anguish, finding pleasure in the excitement of moving from place to place. Child as I was, I at once felt the tenderness and sympathy which endeared Dr. Bell to so many hearts.

He held me on his knee while I examined his watch, and he made it strike for me. He understood my signs, and I knew it and loved him at once. But I did not dream that that interview would be the door through which I should pass from darkness into light, from isolation to friendship, companionship, knowledge, love.

Dr. Bell advised my father to write to Mr. Anagnos, director of the Perkins Institution in Boston, the scene of Dr. Howe's great labors for the blind, and ask him if he had a teacher able to begin my education. This my father did at once. In a few weeks there came a kind letter from Mr. Anagnos with the comforting assurance that a teacher had been found. This was in the summer of 1886, but Miss Sullivan did not arrive until the following March.

Miss Sullivan Comes

The most important day I remember in all my life is the one on which my teacher, Anne Mansfield Sullivan, came to me. I am filled with wonder when I consider the immeasurable contrasts between the two lives that it connects. It was the third of March, 1887, three months before I was seven years old.

On the afternoon of that eventful day, I stood on the porch, expectant. I guessed vaguely from my mother's signs and from the hurrying to and fro in the house that something unusual was about to happen, so I went to the door and waited on the steps. The afternoon sun penetrated the mass of honeysuckle that covered the porch and fell on my upturned face. My fingers lingered almost unconsciously on the familiar leaves and blossoms that had just come forth to greet the sweet southern spring. I did not know what the future held of marvel or surprise for me. Anger and bitterness had preyed upon me continually for weeks and a deep languor had followed this passionate struggle.

Have you ever been at sea in a dense fog, when it seemed as if a tangible white darkness shut you in, and the great ship, tense and anxious, groped her way toward the shore with plummet and sounding-line, and you waited with beating heart for something to happen? I was like that ship before my education began, only I was without compass or sounding-line and had no way of knowing how near the harbor was. "Light! give me light!" was the wordless cry of my soul, and the light of love shone on me in that very hour.

I felt approaching footsteps. I stretched out my hand as I supposed to my mother. Someone took it, and I was caught up and held close in the arms of her who had come to reveal all things to me and, more than all things else, to love me.

The morning after my teacher came, she led me into her room and gave me a doll. The little blind children at the Perkins Institution had sent it and Laura Bridgman had dressed it; but I did not know this until afterward. When I had played with it a little while, Miss Sullivan slowly spelled into my hand the word "d-o-l-l." I was at once interested in this finger play and tried to imitate it. When I finally succeeded in making the letters correctly, I was flushed with childish pride and pleasure. Running downstairs to my mother, I held up my hand and made the letters for doll. I did not know that I was spelling a word or even that words existed; I was simply making my fingers go in monkey-like imitation. In the days that followed, I learned to spell in this uncomprehending way a great many words, among them *pin*, *hat*, *cup*, and a few verbs like *sit*, *stand*, and *walk*. But my teacher had been with me several weeks before I understood that everything has a name.

One day, while I was playing with my new doll, Miss Sullivan put my big rag doll into my lap also, spelled "d-o-l-l" and tried to make me understand that "d-o-l-l" applied to both. Earlier in the day we had had a tussle over the words "m-u-g" and "w-a-t-e-r." Miss Sullivan had tried to impress it upon me that "m-u-g" is *mug* and that "w-a-t-e-r" is *water*, but I persisted in confusing the two. In despair she had dropped the subject for the time, only to renew it at the first opportunity. I became impatient at her repeated attempts and, seizing the new doll, I dashed it upon the floor. I was keenly delighted when I felt the fragments of the broken doll at my feet. Neither sorrow nor regret followed my passionate outburst. I had not loved the doll. In the still, dark world in which I lived there was no strong sentiment or tenderness. I felt my teacher sweep the fragments to one side of the hearth, and I had a sense of satisfaction that the cause of my discomfort was removed. She brought me my hat, and I knew I was going out into the warm sunshine. This thought, if a wordless sensation may be called a thought, made me hop and skip with pleasure.

We walked down the path to the well-house, attracted by the fragrance of the honeysuckle with which it was covered. Some one was drawing water, and my teacher placed my hand under the spout. As the cool stream gushed over one hand, she spelled into the other the word *water*, first slowly, then rapidly. I stood still, my whole attention fixed upon the motions of the fingers. Suddenly I felt a misty consciousness as of something forgotten—a thrill of returning thought; and somehow the mystery of language was revealed to me. I knew then that "w-a-t-e-r" meant the wonderful cool something that was flowing over my hand. That living word awakened my soul, gave it light, hope, joy, set it free! There were barriers still, it is true, but barriers that could in time be swept away.

I left the well-house eager to learn. Everything had a name, and each name gave birth to a new thought. As we returned to the house, every object which I touched seemed to quiver with life. That was because I saw everything with the strange, new sight that had come to me. On entering the door, I remembered the doll I had broken. I felt my way to the hearth and picked up the pieces. I tried vainly to put them together. Then my eyes filled with tears; for I realized what I had done. For the first time I felt repentance and sorrow.

I learned a great many new words that day. I do not remember what they all were; but I do know that *mother*, *father*, *sister*, *teacher* were among them—words that were to make the world blossom for me, "like Aaron's rod, with flowers." It would have been difficult to find a happier child than I was as I lay in my crib at the close of that day and lived over the joys it had brought me, and for the first time longed for a new day to come.

A Crown of Wild Olive

by Rosemary Sutcliff

Alfred Brooks trains rigorously to condition his body and discipline his spirit, to develop stamina and discover what's in his heart. Like Alfred, the two Olympic athletes in this short story train hard, intent on proving something—most of all to themselves. As you read, think about the values that inspire these athletes.

It was still early in the day, but already it was growing hot, the white dry heat of the Greek summer; and the faint off-shore wind that made it bearable had begun to feather the water, breaking and blurring the reflections of the galleys lying at anchor in Pireaus Harbor.

Half of Athens, it seemed, had crowded down to the port to watch the *Paralos*, the State Galley, sail for the Isthmus, taking their finest athletes on the first stage of their journey to Olympia.

Every fourth summer it happened; every fourth summer for more than three hundred years. Nothing was allowed to stand in the way, earthquake or pestilence or even war—even the long and weary war which, after a while of uneasy peace, had broken out again last year between Athens and Sparta.

Back in the spring the Herald had come, proclaiming the Truce of the Games; safe conduct through all lands and across all seas, both for athletes and for those who went to watch them compete. And now, from every Greek state, and from colonies and settlements all around the Mediterranean, the athletes would be gathering. . . .

Aboard the *Paralos* was all the ordered bustle of departure, ropes being cast off, rowers in their places at the oars. The Athenian athletes and their trainers with them had gathered on the afterdeck. Amyntas, son of Ariston, had drawn a little apart from the rest. He was the youngest there, still several months from his eighteenth birthday and somewhat conscious that he had not yet sacrificed his boy's long hair to Apollo, while the rest, even of those entered for the boys' events—you counted as a boy at Olympia until you were twenty—were already short-haired and doing their Military Service. A few of them even had scars gained in border clashes with the Spartans, to prove that their real place, whatever it might be on the race track or in the wrestling pit, was with the men. Amyntas envied them. He was proud that he had been picked so young to run for Athens in the Boys' Double Stade, the Four Hundred Yards. But he was lonely. He was bound in with all the others by their shared training; but they were bound together by something else, by another kind of life, other loyalties and shared experiences and private jokes, from which he was still shut out.

The last ropes holding ship to shore were being cast off now. Fathers and brothers and friends on the jetty were calling last moment advice and good luck wishes. Nobody called to Amyntas, but he turned and looked back to where his father stood among the crowd. Ariston had been a runner too in his day, before a Spartan spear wound had stiffened his left knee and spoiled his own hopes of an Olympic Olive Crown. Everyone said that he and Amyntas were very alike, and looking back now at the slight dark man who still held himself like a runner, Amyntas hoped with a warm rush of pride that they were right. He wished he had said so, before he came aboard. There were so many things he would have liked to have said, but he was even more tongue-tied with his father than he was with the rest of the world when it came to saying the things that mattered. Now as the last ropes fell away, he flung up his hand in salute and tried to put them all into one wordless message. "I'll run the best race that's in me, Father—and if the Gods let me win it, I'll remember that I'm winning for us both."

Among the waving crowd, his father flung up an answering hand, as though he had somehow received the message. The water was widening between ship and shore. The Bos'n struck up the rowing time on his flute, and the rowers bent to their oars, sending the *Paralos* through the water towards the harbor mouth. Soon the crowd on shore was only a shingle of dark and colored and white along the waterfront. But far off beyond the roofs of the warehouses and the covered docks, a flake of light showed where high over Athens the sunlight flashed back from the upraised spear-blade of the great Athene of the Citadel, four miles away.

They were out around the mole now, the one sail broke out from the mast, and they headed for the open gulf.

That night they beached the *Paralos* and made camp on the easternmost point of the long island of Salamis; and not long past noon the next day they went ashore at the Isthmus and took horse for Corinth on the far side, where a second galley was waiting to take them down the coast. At evening on the fifth day they rode down into the shallow valley where Olympian Zeus the Father of Gods and men had his sanctuary and where the Sacred Games were celebrated in his honor.

What with the long journey and the strangeness of everything, Amyntas took in very little of that first evening. They were met and greeted by the Council of the Games, whose president made them a speech of welcome, after which the Chief Herald read them the rules. And afterwards they ate the evening meal in the athletes' mess; food that seemed to have no more taste nor substance than the food one eats in a dream. Then the dream blended away into a dark nothingness of sleep that took Amyntas almost before he had lain down in the narrow stretcher bed in the athletes' lodging, which would be his for the next month.

He woke to the first dappled fingers of sunlight shafting in through the doorway of his cell. They wavered and danced a little, as though broken by the shadows of tree branches. Somewhere farther down the valley a cuckoo was calling, and the world was real again, and his, and new as though it had been born that morning. He rolled over and lay for a few moments, his hands behind his head, looking up at the bare rafters; then shot off the bed and through the doorway in one swallow-dive of movement, to sluice his head and shoulders in the icy water trickling from the mouth of a stone bull into a basin just outside. He came up for air, spluttering and shaking the water out of his eyes. For a moment he saw the colonnaded court and the plane tree arching over the basin through a splintered brightness of flying droplets. And then suddenly, in the brightness, there stood a boy of about his own age, who must have come out of the lodging close behind him. A boy with a lean angular body and a dark, bony face under a shock of hair like the crest of an ill-groomed pony. For a long moment they stood looking at each other. Then Amyntas moved aside to let the other come to the conduit.

As the stranger ducked his head and shoulders under the falling water, Amyntas saw his back. From shoulder to flank it was criss-crossed with scars, past the purple stage but not yet faded to the silvery white that they would be in a few years' time; pinkish scars that looked as though the skin was still drawn uncomfortably tight over them.

He must have made some betraying sound or movement, because the other boy ducked out from under the water, thrusting the wet russet hair back out of his eyes, and demanded curtly, "Have you never seen a Spartan back before?"

So that was it. Amyntas, like everyone else, had heard dark stories of Spartan boys flogged, sometimes to death, in a ritual test of courage before the shrine of Artemis Orthia, the Lady of the Beasts.

"No," he said, "I am Athenian." And did not add that he hoped to see plenty of Spartan backs when once he had started his Military Service. It was odd, the cheap jibe came neatly into his head, and yet he did not even want to speak it. It was as though here at Olympia, the Truce of the Games was not just a rule of conduct, but something in one's heart. Instead, he added, "And my name is Amyntas."

They seemed to stand confronting each other for a long time. The Spartan boy had the look of a dog sniffing at a stranger's fist and taking his own time to make sure whether it was friendly. Then he smiled; a slow, rather grave smile, but unexpectedly warm. "And mine is Leon."

"And you're a runner." Amyntas was taking in his build and the way he stood.

"I am entered for the Double Stade."

"Then we race against each other."

Leon said in the same curt tone, "May we both run a good race."

"And meanwhile,—when did you arrive, Leon?"

"Last night, the same as you."

Amyntas, who usually found it nearly as difficult to talk to strangers as he did to his own father, was surprised to hear himself saying, "Then you'll have seen no more of Olympia than I have. Shall we go and get some clothes on and have a look around?"

But by that time more men and boys were coming out into the early sunshine, yawning and stretching the sleep out of their muscles. And Amyntas felt a hand clamp down on his shoulder and heard the voice of Hippias his trainer, "Oh no you don't, my lad! Five days' break in training is long enough, and I've work for you before you do any sightseeing!"

After that, they were kept hard at it, on the practice track and in the wrestling school that had the names of past Olympic victors carved on the colonnade walls. For the last month's training for the Games had to be done at Olympia itself; and the last month's training was hard, in the old style that did not allow for rest days in the modern fashion that most of the Athenian trainers favored. Everything at Olympia had to be done the old way, even to clearing the stadium of its four years' growth of grass and weeds and spreading it with fresh sand. At other Crown Games, the work was done by paid laborers, but here, the contending athletes must do it themselves, to the glory of the Gods, as they had done it in the far-off days when the Games were new. Some of them grumbled a good deal and thought it was time that the Priests of Zeus and the Council of the Games brought their ideas up to date; but to

Amyntas there seemed to be a sort of rightness about the thing as it was.

His training time was passed among boys from Corinth and Epidauros, Rhodes and Samos and Macedon. At first they were just figures in outline, like people seen too far off to have faces, whom he watched with interest at track work, at javelin or discus throwing or in the wrestling pit, trying to judge their form as he knew they were trying to judge his and each other's. But gradually as the early days went by, they changed into people with faces, with personal habits, and likes and dislikes, suffering from all the strains and stresses of the last weeks before the Games. But even before those first few days were over, he and the Spartan boy had drifted into a companionable pattern of doing things together. They would sluice each other down, squatting in the stone hip-baths in the washing room after practice, and scrape the mess of rubbing oil and sand off each other's backs—it took Amyntas a little while to learn to scrape the bronze blade of the strigil straight over the scars on Leon's back as though they were not there—and when they took their turn at scraping up the four years' growth of grass and sun-dried herbs from the stadium, they generally worked together, sharing one of the big rush carrying-baskets between them. And in the evenings, after the day's training was over, or in the hot noonday break when most people stretched themselves out in the shade of the plane trees for sleep or quiet talk, they seemed, more often than not, to drift into each other's company.

Once or twice they went to have a look at the town of tents and booths that was beginning to spring up all around the Sacred Enclosure and the Gymnasium buildings—for a Games Festival drew many people besides those who came to compete or to watch: merchants and wine sellers and fortune tellers, poets determined to get poems heard, horse dealers from Corinth and Cyrene, goldsmiths and leather-workers, philosophers gathering for the pleasure of arguing with each other, sword and fire swallowers, and acrobats who could dance on their hands to the soft notes of Phrygian pipes. But Leon did not much like the crowded noisy tent-ground; and most often they wandered down to the river that flung its loop about the south side of Olympia. It had shrunk now in the summer heat, to little more than a chain of pools in the middle of its pale dried-out pebbly bed; but there was shade under the oleander trees, and generally a whisper of moving air. And lying on the bank in the shade was free. It had dawned on Amyntas quite early that the reason Leon did not like the fairground was that he had no money. The Spartans did not use money, or at least, having decided that it was a bad thing, they had no coinage but iron bars so big and heavy that nobody could carry them about or even keep a store at home that was worth enough to be any use. They were very proud of their freedom from wealth, but it made life difficult at a gathering such as this, when they had to mix with people from other states. Leon covered up by being extremely scornful of the foolish things for sale in the merchants' booths and the acrobats who passed the bowl around for contributions after their performance; but he was just that shade too scornful to be convincing. And anyway, Amyntas had none too much money himself, to get him through the month.

So they went to the river. They were down there one hot noontide something over a week after they had first arrived at Olympia; Amyntas lying on his back, his hands behind his head, squinting up into the dark shadow-shapes of the oleander branches against the sky; Leon sitting beside him with his arms around his updrawn knees, staring out into the dazzle of sunlight over the open riverbed. They had been talking runners' talk, and suddenly Amyntas said, "I was watching the Corinthian making his practice run this morning. I don't *think* we have either of us much to fear from him."

"The Rhodian runs well," said Leon, not bringing back his gaze from the white dance of sunlight beyond the oleanders.

"But he uses himself up too quickly. He's the kind that makes all the front running at first and has nothing left for the home stretch. Myself, I'd say that red-headed barbarian from Macedon had the better chance."

"He's well enough for speed; and he knows how and when to use it. . . . What do you give for Nikomedes' chances?"

"Nikomedes?—The boy from Megara? It's hard to say. Not much, from the form he's shown so far; but we've only seen him at practice, and he's the sort that sometimes catches fire when it comes to the real thing. . . ."

There was a long silence between them, and they heard the churring of the grasshoppers, like the heat-shimmer turned to sound. And then Amyntas said, "I think you are the one I have most to fear."

And Leon turned his head slowly and looked down at him, and said, "Have you only just woken to that? I knew the same thing of *you*, three days ago."

And they were both silent again and suddenly a little shocked. You might think that kind of thing, but it was best not to put it into words.

Leon made a quick sign with his fingers to avert ill

luck; and Amyntas scrambled to his feet. "Come on, it's time we were getting back." They were both laughing, but a little breathlessly. Leon dived to his feet also and shot ahead as they went up through the riverside scrub. But the next instant, between one flying leap and the next, he stumbled slightly and checked, then turned back, stooping to search for something among the dusty root-tangle of dry grass and camomile. Amyntas, swerving just in time to avoid him, checked also.

"What is it?"

"Something sharp. . . ." Leon pulled out from where it had lain half-buried, the broken end of a sickle blade that looked as though it might have lain there since the last Games. "Seems it's not only the Stadium that needs clearing up." He began to walk on, carrying the jagged fragment in his hand. But Amyntas saw the blood on the dry ground where he had been standing.

"You have cut your foot."

"I know," Leon said, and went on walking.

"Yes, I *know* you know. Let me look at it."

"It's only a scratch."

"All the same—show me."

Leon stood on one leg, steadying himself with a hand on Amyntas's shoulder, and turned up the sole of his foot. "Look then. You can hardly see it."

There was a cut on the hard brown sole, not long, but deep, with the blood welling slowly. Amyntas said in sudden exasperation, "Haven't you *any* sense? Oh we all know about the Spartan boy with the fox under his cloak, and nobody but you Spartans think it's a particularly clever or praiseworthy story; but if you get dirt into that cut, you'll like enough have to scratch from the race!"

Leon suddenly grinned. "Nobody but we Spartans

understand that story. But about the dirt, you could be right."

"I could. And that bit of iron is dirty enough for a start. Best get the wound cleaned up, in the river before we go back to the Gymnasium. Then your trainer can take over."

So with Leon sitting on a boulder at the edge of the shrunken river, Amyntas set to work with ruthless thoroughness to clean the cut. He pulled it open, the cool water running over his hands, and a thin thread of crimson fronded away downstream. It would help clean the wound to let it bleed a little; but after a few moments the bleeding almost stopped. No harm in making sure; he ducked his head to the place, sucked hard and spat crimson into the water. Then he tore a strip from the skirt of his tunic. He would have commandeered Leon's own—after all it was Leon's foot—but he knew that the Spartan boys were allowed to own only one tunic at a time. If he did that, Leon would be left without a respectable tunic to wear at the Sacrifices. He lashed the thin brown foot tightly. "Now—put your arm over my shoulder and try to keep your weight off the cut as much as you can."

"Cluck, cluck, cluck!" said Leon, but he did as Amyntas said.

As they skirted the great open space of the Hippodrome, where the chariot races would be held on the second day of the Games, they came up with a couple of the Athenian contingent, strolling under the plane trees. Eudorus the wrestler looked around and his face quickened with concern, "Run into trouble?"

"Ran into the remains of a sickle blade someone left in the long grass," Amyntas said, touching the rusty bit of metal he had taken from Leon and stuck in his own belt. "It's near the tendon, but it's all right, so long as there's no dirt left in it."

"Near the tendon, eh? Then we'd best be taking no chances." Eudorus looked at Leon. "You are Spartan, I think?—Amyntas, go and find the Spartan trainer. I'll take over here." And then to Leon again, "Will you allow me to carry you up to the lodging? It seems the simplest way."

Amyntas caught one parting glimpse of Leon's rigid face as Eudorus lifted him, lightly as a ten-year-old, and set off towards the gymnasium buildings; and laughter caught at his stomach; but mixed with the laughter was sympathy. He knew he would have been just as furious in Leon's place. All this fuss and to-do over a cut that would have been nothing in itself—if the Games had not been only three weeks off.

He set off in search of the trainer.

In the middle of that night, Amyntas woke up with a thought already shaped and complete in his mind. It was an ugly thought, and it sat on his chest and mouthed at him slyly. "Leon is the one you have most to fear. If Leon is out of the race. . . ."

He looked at it in the darkness, feeling a little sick. Then he pushed it away and rolled over on to his face with his head in his arms, and after a while he managed to go back to sleep again.

Next day, as soon as he could slip away between training sessions, he went out into the growing town of tents and booths, and found a seller of images and votive offerings, and bought a little bronze bull with silvered horns. It cost nearly all the money that he had to spare, so that he would not now be able to buy the hunting knife with silver inlay on the hilt that had caught his fancy a day or two since. With the little figure in his hand, he went to the Sacred Enclosure, where, among altars shaded by plane trees and statues of Gods and Olympic heroes, the great Temple of Zeus faced the older and darker house of Hera his wife.

Before the Temple of Zeus, the ancient wild olive trees from which the victors' crowns were made cast dapple-shade across the lower steps of the vast portico. He spoke to the attendant priest in the deep threshold shadows beyond.

"I ask leave to enter and make an offering."

"Enter then, and make the offering," the man said.

And he went through into the vastness of the Temple itself, where the sunlight sifting through under the acanthus roof tiles made a honeycomb glow that hung high in the upper spaces and flowed down the gigantic columns but scarcely touched the pavement under foot, so that he seemed to wade in cool shadows. At the far end, sheathed in gold and ivory, his feet half lost in shadows, his head gloried with the dim radiance of the upper air, stern and serene above the affairs of mortal men, stood the mighty statue of the God himself. Olympian Zeus, in whose honor the Sacred Games had been held for more than three hundred years. Three hundred years, such a little while; looking up at the heart-stilling face above him, Amyntas wondered if the God had even noticed yet, that they were begun. Everything in the God's House was so huge, even time. . . . For a moment his head swam, and he had no means of judging the size of anything, even himself, here where all the known landmarks of the world of men were left behind. Only one thing, when he looked down at it, remained constant in size; the tiny bronze bull with the silvered horns that he held in his hand.

He went forward to the first of the Offering Tables

before the feet of the gigantic statue and set it down. Now, the tables were empty and waiting, but by the end of the festival, they would be piled with offerings; small humble ones like his own and silver cups and tripods of gilded bronze to be taken away and housed in the Temple treasury. On the eve of the Games they would begin to fill up, with votive offerings made for the most part by the athletes themselves, for their own victory or the victory of a friend taking part in a different event. Amyntas was not making the offering for his own victory, nor for Leon's. He was not quite sure why he was making it, but it was for something much more complicated than victory in the Double Stade. With one finger still resting on the back of the little bronze bull, he sent up the best prayer he could sort out from the tangle of thoughts and feelings within himself. "Father of all things, Lord of these Sacred Games, let me keep a clean heart in this; let me run the best race that is in me and think of nothing more."

Outside again, beyond the dapple-shade of the olive trees, the white sunlight fell dazzling across his eyes, and the world of men, in which things had returned to their normal size, received him back; and he knew that Hippias was going to be loudly angry with him for having missed a training session. But unaccountably, everything, including Hippias's anger, seemed surprisingly small.

Leon had to break training for three days, at least so far as track-work was concerned; and it was several more before he could get back into full training; so for a while it was doubtful whether he would be able to take his place in the race. But with still more than a week to go, both his trainer and the Doctor-Priest of Asklepius declared him fit, and his name remained on the list of entrants for the Double Stade.

And then it was the first day of the Festival; the day of solemn dedication, when each competitor must go before the Council to be looked over and identified and take the Oath of the Games before the great bronze statue of Zeus of the Thunderbolts.

The day passed. And next morning before it was light, Amyntas woke to hear the unmistakable, unforgettable voice of the crowds gathering in the Stadium. A shapeless surf of sound, pricked by the sharper cries of the jugglers and acrobats, and the sellers of water and honeycakes, myrtle and victors' ribbons calling their wares.

This was the day of the Sacred Procession; the Priests and Officials, the beasts garlanded for sacrifice, the athletes marching into the waiting Stadium, while the Herald proclaimed the name and state of each one as he passed the rostrum. Amyntas, marching in with the Athenians, heard his own name called, and Leon's, among names from Samos and Cyrene, Crete and Corinth, and Argos and Megara. And he smelled the incense on the morning air and felt for the first time, under his swelling pride in being Athenian, the thread of his own Greekness interwoven with the Greekness of all those others. This must have been, a little, the thing their Great-Grandfathers had felt when they stood together, shield to shield, to hurl back the whole strength of invading Persia so that they might remain free. That had been in a Games year, too. . . .

The rest of that day was given over to the chariot and horse races; and that night Amyntas went to his sleeping cell with the thunder of hooves and wheels still sounding somewhere behind his ears. He seemed to hear it in his dreams all night, but when he woke in the morning, it had turned into the sound that he had woken to yesterday, the surf-sound of the gathering crowd. But this morning it had a new note for him, for this was the Day, and the crowd that was gathering out there around the Stadium was his crowd, and his belly tightened and the skin prickled at the back of his neck as he heard it.

He lay for a few moments, listening, then got up and went out to the conduit. Leon came out after him as he had done that first morning of all, and they sluiced down as best they could. The water barely dribbled from the mouth of the stone bull now, for with the vast gathering of people and the usual end-of-summer drought, the water shortage was getting desperate, as it always did by the time the Festival days arrived.

"How is the foot?" Amyntas asked.

"I can't remember where the cut was, unless I look for it."

They stood looking at each other, the friendship that they had never put into words trying to find some way to reach across from one to the other.

"We cannot even wish each other luck," Amyntas said at last, helplessly.

And Leon said, almost exactly as he had said it at their first meeting, "May both of us run a good race."

They reached out and touched hands quickly and went their separate ways.

The next time they saw each other, they were waiting oiled and naked for the track, with the rest of the Double Stade boys just outside the arched way into the Stadium. The Dolichus, the long distance race, and the Stade had been run, each with its boys' race immediately after. Now the trumpet was sounding to start the Double Stade. Amyntas's eyes went to meet Leon's, and found the Spartan boy's slightly frowning gaze waiting for him. He heard the sudden roar of the crowd, and his belly lifted and tightened. A little stir ran through the waiting boys; the next time the starting trumpet sounded, the next time the crowd gave that roar, it would be for them. Hippias was murmuring last-minute advice into Amyntas's ear, but he did not hear a word of it. . . . He was going out there before all those thousands upon thousands of staring eyes and yelling mouths, and he was going to fail. Not just fail to win the race, but *fail*. His belly was churning now, his heart banging away right up in his throat so that it almost choked him. His mouth was dry and the palms of his hands were wet, and the beginnings of panic were whimpering up in him. He looked again at Leon and saw him run the tip of his tongue over his lips as though they were suddenly dry. It was the first time he had ever known the Spartan boy to betray anything of what was going on inside him, and the sight gave him a sense of companionship that somehow steadied him. He began to take deep quiet breaths, as he had been taught, and the rising panic quieted and sank away.

The voice of the crowd was rising, rising to a great roar; the Men's Double Stade was over. He heard the Herald crying the name of the winner and another roar from the crowd; and then the runners were coming out through the arched entrance; and the boys pressed back to let them past, filthy with sweat and sand and oil. Amyntas looked at the face of the man with the victor's ribbons knotted around his head and arms and saw that it was grey and spent and oddly peaceful.

"Now it's us!" someone said; and the boys were sprinting down the covered way, out into the open sun-drenched space of the Stadium.

The turf banks on either side of the broad track and the lower slopes of the Kronon Hill that looked down upon it were packed with a vast multitude of onlookers. Half-way down on the right-hand side, raised above the tawny grass on which everybody else sat, were the benches for the Council, looking across to the white marble seat opposite, where the Priestess of Demeter, the only woman allowed at the Games, sat as still as though she herself were carved from marble, among all the jostling, swaying, noisy throng. Men were raking over the silver sand on the track. The trumpeter stood ready.

They had taken their places now behind the long white limestone curbs of the starting line. The Umpire was calling: "Runners! Feet to the lines!"

Amyntas felt the scorching heat of the limestone as he braced the ball of his right foot into the shaped groove. All the panic of a while back had left him; he felt light, and clearheaded, and master of himself. He had drawn the sixth place, with Leon on his left and the boy from Megara on his right. Before him the track stretched white in the sunlight, an infinity of emptiness and distance.

The starting trumpet yelped, and the line of runners sprang forward like a wave of hunting dogs slipped from the leash.

Amyntas was running smoothly and without hurry. Let the green front-runners push on ahead. In this heat they would have burned themselves out before they reached the turning post. He and Leon were running neck and neck with the red-headed Macedonian. The Rhodian had gone ahead now after the front-runners; the rest were still bunched. Then the Corinthian made a sprint and passed the boy from Rhodes, but fell back almost at once. The white track was reeling back underfoot, the turning post racing towards them. The bunch had thinned out, the front-runners beginning to drop back already; and as they came up towards the turning post, the first boy from Macedon, and then Nikomedes catching fire at last, slid into the lead, with Amyntas and Leon close behind them. Rounding the post, Amyntas skidded on the loose sand and Leon went ahead; and it was then, seeing the lean scarred back ahead of him, that Amyntas lengthened his stride, knowing that the time had come to run. They were a quarter of the way down the home lap when they passed Nikomedes; the Megaran boy had taken fire too late. They were beginning to overhaul the redhead; and Amyntas knew in his bursting heart that unless something unexpected happened, the race must be between himself and Leon. Spartan and Macedonian were going neck and neck now; the position held for a few paces, and then the redhead gradually fell behind. Amyntas was going all out. There was pain in his breast and belly and in the backs of his legs, and he did not know where his next breath was coming from; but still the thin scarred back was just ahead. And then suddenly Amyntas knew that something was wrong; Leon was laboring a little, beginning to lose the first keen edge of his speed. Snatching a glance downward, he saw a fleck of crimson in the sand. The cut had reopened.

His body went on running, but for a sort of splinter of time his head seemed quite apart from the rest of him and filled with an unmanageable swirl of thoughts and feelings. Leon might have passed the top of his speed anyway; it might be nothing to do with his foot—But the cut *had* reopened. . . . To lose the race because of a cut foot. . . . It would be so easy not to make that final desperate effort that his whole body was crying out against. Then Leon would keep his lead. . . . And at the same time another part of himself was remembering his father standing on the quayside at Piraeus as the *Paralos* drew away— crying out that he was not running only for himself but for Athens, his City and his people. . . . A crown of wild olive would be the greatest thing that anyone could give to his friend. . . . It would insult Leon to let him win . . . you could not do that to your friend. . . . And then, like a clean cold sword of light cutting through the swirling tangle of his thoughts, came the knowledge that greater than any of these things were the Gods. These were the Sacred Games, not some mere struggle between boys in the gymnasium. For one fleeting instant of time, he remembered himself standing in the Temple before the great statue of Zeus, holding the tiny bronze bull with the silvered horns. "Let me run the best race that is in me and think of nothing more."

He drove himself forward in one last agonizing burst of speed. He was breathing against knives, and the roar of the blood in his ears drowned the roar of the crowd. He was level with Leon—and then there was nothing ahead of him but the winning post.

The onlookers had crowded right down towards it; even above the howl of the blood in his head he heard them now, roar on solid roar of sound, shouting him in to victory. And then Hippias had caught him as he plunged past the post; and he was bending over the trainer's arm, bending over the pain in his belly, snatching at his breath and trying not to be sick. People were throwing sprigs of myrtle; he felt them flicking and falling on his head and shoulders. The sickness eased a little and his head was clearing; he began to hear friendly voices congratulating him; and Eudorus came shouldering through the crowd with a colored ribbon to tie around his head. But when he looked around for Leon, the Spartan boy had been swept away by his trainer. And a desolation rose in Amyntas and robbed his moment of its glory.

Afterwards in the changing room, some of the other boys came up to congratulate him. Leon did not come; but when they had cleaned off the sand and oil and sweat and sluiced down with the little water that was allowed them, Amyntas hung about, sitting on the well curb outside while the trainer finished seeing to his friend's foot. And when Leon came out at last, he came straight across to the well, as though they had arranged to meet there. His face was as unreadable as usual.

"You will have cooled off enough by now. Do you want to drink?" Amyntas said, mainly because somebody had to say something, and dipped the bronze cup that always stood on the well curb in the pail that he had drawn.

Leon took the cup from him and drank and sat down on the well curb beside him. As Amyntas dipped the cup again and bent his head to drink in his turn, the ends of the victor's ribbon fell forward against his cheek, and he pulled it off impatiently and dropped it beside the well.

"Why did you do that?" Leon said.

"I shall never be sure whether I won that race."

"The judges are not often mistaken, and I never heard yet of folk tying victors' ribbons on the wrong man."

Amyntas flicked a thumb at Leon's bandaged foot. "You know well enough what I mean. I'll never be sure whether I'd have come first past the post, if that hadn't opened up again."

Leon looked at him a moment in silence, then flung up his head and laughed. "Do you really think that could make any difference? It would take more than a cut foot to slow me up, Athenian!—You ran the better race, that's all."

It was said on such a harsh, bragging note that in the first moment Amyntas felt as though he had been struck in the face. Then he wondered if it was the overwhelming Spartan pride talking or simply Leon, hurt and angry and speaking the truth. Either way, he was too tired to be angry back again. And whichever it was it seemed that Leon had shaken it off already. The noon break was over, and the trumpets were sounding for the Pentathlon.

"Up!" Leon said, when Amyntas did not move at once. "Are you going to let it be said that your own event is the only one that interests you?"

They went, quickly and together, while the trainer's eye was off them, for Leon was under orders to keep off his foot. And the people cheered them both when they appeared in the Stadium. They seldom cared much for a good loser, but Leon had come in a close second, and they had seen the blood in the sand.

The next day the heavyweight events were held; and then it was the last day of all, the Crowning Day. Ever after, Amyntas remembered that day as a quietness after great stress and turmoil. It was not, in truth, much less noisy than the days that had gone before. The roaring of the Stadium crowds was gone, but in the town of tents the crowds milled to and fro. The jugglers with knives and the eaters of fire shouted for an audience and the merchants cried their wares, and within the Sacred Enclosure where the winners received their crowns and made their sacrifices before the Temples of Zeus and Hera, there were the flutes and the songs in praise of the victors and the deep-voiced invocations to the Gods.

But in Amyntas himself, there was the quiet. He remembered the Herald crying his name and the light springy coolness of the wild olive crown as it was pressed down on his head; and later, the spitting light of pine torches under the plane trees, where the officials and athletes were feasting. And he remembered most, looking up out of the torchlight, and seeing, high and remote above it all, the winged tripods on the roof of the great Temple, outlined against the light of a moon two days past the full.

The boys left before the feasting was over; and in his sleeping cell Amyntas heard the poets sing in praise of some chariot team and the applause, while he gathered his few belongings together, ready for tomorrow's early start, and stowed his olive crown among them. Already the leaves were beginning to wilt after the heat of the day. The room that had seemed so strange the first night was familiar now, part of himself; and after tonight it would not know him anymore.

Next morning in all the hustle of departure, he and Leon contrived to meet and slip off for a little on their own.

The whole valley of Olympia was a chaos of tents and booths being taken down, merchants as well as athletes and onlookers making ready for the road. But the Sacred Enclosure itself was quiet, and the gates stood open. They went through, into the shade of the olive trees before the Temple of Zeus. A priest making the morning offering at a side altar looked at them; but they seemed to be doing no harm and to want nothing, so he let them alone. There was a smell of frankincense in the air and the early morning smell of last night's heavy dew on parched ground. They stood among the twisted trunks and low-hanging branches and looked at each other and did not know what to say. Already they were remembering that there was war between Athens and Sparta, that the Truce of the Games would last them back to their own states, but no further; and the longer the silence lasted, the more they remembered.

From beyond the quiet of the Enclosure came all the sounds of the great concourse breaking up; voices calling, the stamping of impatient horses. "By this time tomorrow everyone will be gone," Amyntas said at last. "It will be just as it was before we came, for another four years."

"The Corinthians are off already."

"Catching the cool of the morning for those fine chariot horses," Amyntas said, and thought, There's so little time, why do we have to waste it like this?

"One of the charioteers had that hunting knife with the silver inlay. The one you took a fancy to. Why didn't you buy it after all?"

"I spent the money on something else." For a moment Amyntas was afraid that Leon would ask what. But the other boy only nodded and let it go.

He wished suddenly that he could give Leon something, but there was nothing among his few belongings that would make sense in the Spartan's world. It was a world so far off from his own. Too far to reach out, too far to call. Already they seemed to be drifting away from each other, drifting back to a month ago, before they had even met. He put out a hand quickly, as though to hold the other boy back for one more moment, and Leon's hand came to meet it.

"It has been good. All this month it has been good," Leon said.

"It has been good," Amyntas agreed. He wanted

to say, "Until the next Games, then." But manhood and Military Service were only a few months away for both of them. If they did meet at another Games, there would be the faces of dead comrades, Spartan or Athenian, between them; and like enough, for one of them or both, there might be no other Games. Far more likely, if they ever saw each other again, it would be over the tops of their shields.

He had noticed before how, despite their different worlds, he and Leon sometimes thought the same thing at the same time and answered each other as though the thought had been spoken. Leon said in his abrupt, dead-level voice, "The Gods be with you, Amyntas, and grant that we never meet again."

They put their arms around each other's necks and strained fiercely close for a moment, hard cheekbone against hard cheekbone.

"The Gods be with you, Leon."

And then Eudorus was calling, "Amyntas! Amyntas! We're all waiting!"

And Amyntas turned and ran—out through the gateway of the Sacred Enclosure, towards where the Athenian party were ready to start, and Eudorus was already coming back to look for him.

As they rode up from the Valley of Olympia and took the tracks towards the coast, Amyntas did not look back. The horses' legs brushed the dry dust-grey scrub beside the track and loosed the hot aromatic scents of wild lavender and camomile and lentisk upon the air. A yellow butterfly hovered past, and watching it out of sight, it came to him suddenly that he and Leon had exchanged gifts of a sort, after all. It was hard to give them a name, but they were real enough. And the outward and visible sign of his gift to Leon was in the little bronze bull with the silvered horns that he had left on the Offering Table before

the feet of Olympian Zeus. And Leon's gift to him.
. . . That had been made with the Spartan's boast that
it would take more than a cut foot to slow him up.
He had thought at the time that it was either the
harsh Spartan pride or the truth spoken in anger. But
he understood now, quite suddenly, that it had been
Leon giving up his own private and inward claim to
the olive crown, so that he, Amyntas, might believe
that he had rightfully won it. Amyntas knew that he
would never be sure of that, never in all his life. But
it made no difference to the gift.

The track had begun to run downhill, and the pale
dust-cloud was rising behind them. He knew that if
he looked back now, there would be nothing to see.

The Rights to the Streets of Memphis

by Richard Wright

What is the best way to deal with a bully who is making your life miserable? Many people have had to face this issue. Alfred Brooks, as you recall, has to find a way to deal with Major, a bully in his Harlem neighborhood. In this excerpt from his autobiography, Richard Wright describes a lesson he learned about one way to handle "tough kids" who terrorize others.

Hunger stole upon me so slowly that at first I was not aware of what hunger really meant. Hunger had always been more or less at my elbow when I played, but now I began to wake up at night to find hunger standing at my bedside, staring at me gauntly. The hunger I had known before this had been no grim, hostile stranger; it had been a normal hunger that had made me beg constantly for bread, and when I ate a crust or two I was satisfied. But this new hunger baffled me, scared me, made me angry and insistent. Whenever I begged for food now, my mother would pour me a cup of tea which would still the clamor in my stomach for a moment or two; but a little later I would feel hunger nudging my ribs, twisting my empty guts until they ached. I would grow dizzy and my vision would dim. I became less active in my play, and for the first time in my life, I had to pause and think of what was happening to me.

"Mama, I'm hungry," I complained one afternoon.

"Jump up and catch a kungry," she said, trying to make me laugh and forget.

"What's a 'kungry'?"

"It's what little boys eat when they get hungry," she said.

"What does it taste like?"

"I don't know."

"Then why do you tell me to catch one?"

"Because you said that you were hungry," she said, smiling.

I sensed that she was teasing me, and it made me angry.

"But I'm hungry. I want to eat."

"You'll have to wait."

"But I want to eat now."

"But there's nothing to eat," she told me.

"Why?"

"Just because there's none," she explained.

"But I want to eat," I said, beginning to cry.

"You'll just have to wait," she said again.

"But why?"

"For God to send some food."

"When is He going to send it?"

"I don't know."

"But I'm hungry!"

She was ironing, and she paused and looked at me with tears in her eyes.

"Where's your father?" she asked me.

I stared in bewilderment. Yes, it was true that my father had not come home to sleep for many days now, and I could make as much noise as I wanted. Though I had not known why he was absent, I had been glad that he was not there to shout his restrictions at me. But it had never occurred to me that his absence would mean that there would be no food.

"I don't know," I said.

"Who brings food into the house?" my mother asked me.

"Papa," I said. "He always brought food."

"Well, your father isn't here now," she said.

"Where is he?"

"I don't know," she said.

"But I'm hungry," I whimpered, stomping my feet.

"You'll have to wait until I get a job and buy food," she said.

As the days slid past, the image of my father became associated with my pangs of hunger, and whenever I felt hunger, I thought of him with a deep, biological bitterness.

My mother finally went to work as a cook and left me and my brother alone in the flat each day with a loaf of bread and a pot of tea. When she returned at evening, she would be tired and dispirited and would cry a lot. Sometimes, when she was in despair, she would call us to her and talk to us for hours, telling us that we now had no father, that our lives would be different from those of other children, that we must learn as soon as possible to take care of ourselves, to dress ourselves, to prepare our own food; that we must take upon ourselves the responsibility of the flat while she worked. Half-frightened, we would promise solemnly. We did not understand what had happened between our father and our mother, and the most that these long talks did to us was to make us feel a vague dread. Whenever we asked why father had left, she would tell us that we were too young to know.

One evening my mother told me that thereafter I would have to do the shopping for food. She took me to the corner store to show me the way. I was proud; I felt like a grown-up. The next afternoon I looped the basket over my arm and went down the pavement toward the store. When I reached the corner, a gang of boys grabbed me, knocked me down, snatched the basket, took the money, and sent me running home in panic. That evening I told my mother what had happened, but she made no comment; she sat down at once, wrote another note, gave me more money, and sent me out to the grocery again. I crept down the steps and saw the same gang of boys playing down the street. I ran back into the house.

"What's the matter?" my mother asked.

"It's those same boys," I said. "They'll beat me."

"You've got to get over that," she said. "Now, go on."

"I'm scared," I said.

"Go on and don't pay any attention to them," she said.

I went out of the door and walked briskly down the sidewalk, praying that the gang would not molest me. But when I came abreast of them, someone shouted.

"There he is!"

They came toward me and I broke into a wild run toward home. They overtook me and flung me to the pavement. I yelled, pleaded, kicked, but they wrenched the money out of my hand. They yanked me to my feet, gave me a few slaps, and sent me home sobbing. My mother met me at the door.

"They b-beat m-me," I gasped. "They t-t-took the m-money."

I started up the steps, seeking the shelter of the house.

"Don't you come in here," my mother warned me.

I froze in my tracks and stared at her.

"But they're coming after me," I said.

"You just stay right where you are," she said in a deadly tone. "I'm going to teach you this night to stand up and fight for yourself."

She went into the house, and I waited, terrified, wondering what she was about. Presently she returned with more money and another note; she also had a long, heavy stick.

"Take this money, this note, and this stick," she said. "Go to the store and buy those groceries. If those boys bother you, then fight."

I was baffled. My mother was telling me to fight, a thing that she had never done before.

"But I'm scared," I said.

"Don't you come into this house until you've gotten those groceries," she said.

"They'll beat me; they'll beat me," I said.

"Then stay in the streets; don't come back here!"

I ran up the steps and tried to force my way past her into the house. A stinging slap came on my jaw. I stood on the sidewalk, crying.

"Please, let me wait until tomorrow," I begged.

"No," she said. "Go now! If you come back into this house without those groceries, I'll whip you!"

She slammed the door and I heard the key turn in the lock. I shook with fright. I was alone upon the dark, hostile streets, and gangs were after me. I had the choice of being beaten at home or away from home. I clutched the stick, crying, trying to reason. If I were beaten at home, there was absolutely nothing that I could do about it; but if I were beaten in the streets, I had a chance to fight and defend myself. I walked slowly down the sidewalk, coming closer to the gang of boys, holding the stick tightly. I was so full of fear that I could scarcely breathe. I was almost upon them now.

"There he is again!" the cry went up.

They surrounded me quickly and began to grab for my hand.

"I'll kill you!" I threatened.

They closed in. In blind fear I let the stick fly, feeling it crack against a boy's skull. I swung again, lamming another skull, then another. Realizing that they would retaliate if I let up for but a second, I fought to lay them low, to knock them cold, to kill them so that they could not strike back at me. I flayed with tears in my eyes, teeth clenched, stark fear making me throw every ounce of my strength behind each blow. I hit again and again, dropping the money and the grocery list. The boys scattered, yelling, nursing their heads, staring at me in utter disbelief. They had never seen such frenzy. I stood panting, egging them on, taunting them to come on and fight. When they refused, I ran after them and they tore out for their homes, screaming. The parents of the boys rushed into the streets and threatened me, and for the first time in my life I shouted at grown-ups, telling them that I would give them the same if they bothered me. I finally found my grocery list and the money and went to the store. On my way back I kept my stick poised for instant use, but there was not a single boy in sight. That night I won the right to the streets of Memphis.

Joan Benoit:
1984 U.S. Olympic Marathon Gold Medalist

by Rina Ferrarelli

*What happens when you dedicate yourself
to being the best you can be at a sport or
an activity? What inner qualities do you
develop? As you read this poem, think
about the qualities that the speaker
admires in Joan Benoit. Then compare
those qualities with Alfred's.*

During the third mile
not the eighteenth as expected
she surged ahead
leaving behind the press
5   of bodies, the breath
hot on her back
and set a pace
the experts claimed
she couldn't possibly keep
10 to the end.

Sure, determined,
moving to an inner rhythm
measuring herself against herself
alone in a field of fifty
15 she gained the twenty-six miles
of concrete, asphalt and humid weather
and burst into the roar of the crowd
to run the lap around the stadium

at the same pace
20   once to finish the race
and then again in victory

and she was still fresh
and not even out of breath
and standing.

Muhammad Ali

by Bill Littlefield

*One of boxing's all-time greats,
Muhammad Ali attracted legions of
admirers—and scores of critics. As you
read this biography, consider what you
learn about Ali as a boxer and as a person.*

"BIBBITY-BIBBITY-BIBBITY-BIBBITY-BAP! bap!
bap! bap!"

In a corner of the Miami gym, the slender young
heavyweight drilled the speed bag. Veterans of the
fight game and tourists alike marveled at the
quickness of his hands.

"Who is he?" asked one.

"Why, that's Cassius Clay," said another. "He won
a gold medal in the Olympics in 1960."

"He's beautiful," the first said, and that was true.
The fighter's face was unmarked and classically
handsome. He said it himself all the time.

"Who's he gonna fight?"

"He's fighting Sonny Liston for the heavyweight
championship of the world," the fight fan said.

"Oh, dear," came the reply. "What a terrible
shame."

When Cassius Clay, later and ever after known as
Muhammad Ali, stepped into the ring on the evening
of February 25, 1964, 93 percent of the sportswriters
in attendance expected him to be nothing more than
a footnote to the violent career of Sonny Liston when
the night was done. At best, they figured he'd be a
noisy footnote. Clay had seen to *that* at the weigh-in,

the prefight ceremony which requires each fighter to step on a scale and had never before amounted to much else. This time it was different. Cassius Clay, the twenty-two-year-old challenger, had entered the room screaming, "I am the champ! I'm ready to rumble! Round eight to prove I'm great! Bring that big ugly bear on!"

Nobody at the weigh-in had ever seen anything like it. More than one writer was convinced that young Clay was crazy, and the physician in attendance figured the fighter was scared to death. Some wondered if Clay would even show up for the actual bout. But a few say now that they saw him wink, and realized even then that Clay was putting on a show.

It was nothing to the show he would put on when the bell rang. Through the first two rounds Clay danced, frustrating Liston, who could not catch up to him to hit him. In the third round the attack began, and Clay opened up a gash under Liston's right eye. Observers at ringside looked at each other in disbelief. When had any of them ever seen the invincible Liston cut before? And when had his own attempts to hit an opponent been so futile? He looked as if he were trying to catch the wind.

But this fight would not be a simple matter of youth versus age or speed versus power. Toward the end of round four, Clay suddenly started having trouble with his eyes. When the round was over he returned to his corner shouting that something was stinging them. "I can't see," he screamed to his trainer, Angelo Dundee. "Cut the gloves off! We're going home!"

But Dundee wasn't quite willing to go along. What the heck . . . his guy seemed to be winning the fight. Maybe he could do something for the eyes. He wiped them with a sponge, dried them, rinsed them out again. When the bell rang to begin round five, Clay's eyes were still tearing. But Dundee shoved the fighter's mouthpiece back in, stood him up, and shouted, "This is the big one, daddy. Stay away from him. Run!"

Clay "ran" for about a minute and a half of round five, and then his eyes cleared. Whatever had been stinging him—maybe something Liston's handlers had been putting on his cuts—was gone. In round six Clay tattooed the champion at will, and Liston couldn't touch him. When the bell rang to start the seventh round, Liston wouldn't answer it. Later he said he'd injured his shoulder and could no longer fight. In any case and against all odds, Cassius Clay was now the heavyweight champion of the world.

Even larger surprises followed. At a press conference the day after the Liston fight, the new champion told reporters, "I know where I'm going and I know the truth, and I don't have to be what you want me to be. I'm free to be what I want."

In that moment, sports fans became aware of the ongoing transformation of Cassius Clay into Muhammad Ali, the man who would not only set the world of boxing on its ear by winning the heavyweight championship two more times, but who would also outrage the American establishment and eventually charm millions of people all over the globe.

Nobody could have seen all that coming in 1964, though hindsight helps make sense of Muhammad Ali's remarkable journey. As a boy growing up in Louisville, Kentucky, he'd assimilated the system of racial segregation that nearly everyone in the American South then took for granted. He'd heard and never forgotten the story of Emmett Till, a black youngster murdered by white men in Mississippi for whistling at a white woman. In 1960 he'd returned with a gold medal from the Olympics in Rome to find that there were still places in his hometown where he could not eat lunch because he was black, albeit an American champion. And eventually, during the early sixties, he'd found a faith to help him understand and stand up to these conditions. The speech the new heavyweight champion made to the press after he'd beaten Sonny Liston was the beginning of Muhammad Ali's declaration of his allegiance to the Nation of Islam, a religion headed in the United States at that time by Elijah Muhammad.

Elijah Muhammad referred to white people as "devils" who had enslaved black Americans for centuries and were still doing so. Muhammad Ali never entirely accepted this characterization, but sportswriters and others were outraged by the new champion's association with the Nation of Islam. His kindest critics called him a fool.

On May 25, 1965, the young champion gave Sonny Liston the customary rematch in Lewiston, Maine. The fight went down in history as the one you missed if you blinked. Muhammad Ali knocked out Sonny Liston in the first round, before many of those who'd come to watch the bout had taken their seats.

For the next two years, Ali defended his championship against all comers. He beat Floyd Patterson in the United States, George Chuvalo in Canada, and Henry Cooper in England, among others. But during those years another opponent was emerging, and this would be one even Ali could not knock out. Throughout the decade of the 1960s, the

United States had been sending soldiers to Southeast Asia to fight in a war in Vietnam. Some of the young men who fought in the war went voluntarily, because they felt it was their duty to serve when their country was involved in a war. But many of the American soldiers in Vietnam were drafted, and many of the draftees were black and poor. Elijah Muhammad, among others, felt this was completely unjust. Why should young black men fight for a country that discriminated against them? Muhammad Ali agreed, and when the United States Government tried to force him to serve in the army, he told them, "I ain't got no quarrel with the Viet Cong." In a quieter moment later on, he referred to his work as a minister in the Muslim faith, the faith embraced by the Nation of Islam. "My faith prohibits me from fighting in the war," Ali contended, "just as it requires me to pray five times a day. How can I kill somebody when I pray five times a day for peace?"

The government didn't see the contradiction, and although there was a provision in the law allowing for the release from military service of young men whose consciences or religious convictions made going to war impossible for them, Muhammad Ali was brought to trial for refusing to join the army. Almost immediately he was stripped of the heavyweight championship and prohibited from boxing. He would be banned from the ring for three and a half years, until the United States Supreme Court could finally reverse the conviction. In other words, Muhammad Ali was denied the opportunity to box until one court could rule that another court, as well as every boxing commission across the country, had been wrong.

Boxing is a terrible way to make a living. Almost nobody who boxes for long comes away from it without eye damage, ear damage, kidney damage, or brain damage. But the attraction of the sport for those who follow it is the purity of courage at its center. Many of the people who promote the fights may be liars and crooks, but once the bell has rung, the contest between two fighters gives each the opportunity to test his strength, his endurance, and his nerve. Muhammad Ali had never lacked any of these qualities in the ring, but now circumstances forced him to find another kind of courage. If he'd agreed to go into the army, he would almost certainly have been safe from harm. As a celebrity, the heavyweight champion, he'd have traveled from military base to military base entertaining the troops with boxing exhibitions. Perhaps he'd have been asked to speak publicly in support of the war. Probably he'd have been free to continue earning his living in the ring. But Muhammad Ali chose the more difficult alternative, the alternative of conscience, and he paid the price for that choice.

By the time Ali was allowed to return to the ring in 1970, a great many people in the United States had decided for a great many reasons that the war in Vietnam was wrong. Many hundreds of thousands had marched in Washington to protest the continuation of the war. And Muhammad Ali himself had become for many folks, black and white, a hero, a fellow who'd shown others how to stand up for themselves and their beliefs.

Back in the ring, he went about trying to do what such great heavyweights as Jack Johnson and Joe Louis had never managed to do: to regain the championship title. His first opportunity to do so came against Joe Frazier, a powerful and relentless puncher. The two met on March 8, 1971, in New York's Madison Square Garden. They hammered each other for fifteen rounds, and in the end the judges declared Frazier the winner. Observers of the fight saw with dismay that during the three and a half years away from the ring Ali had lost a good deal of his foot speed. He could still punch, as indicated by Frazier's battered face, but he could no longer dance away from his opponent's punches as he had once done. He could no longer escape harm as often as he had in the early years. And the longer he fought, the greater the risk of lasting damage would become. Ali must have understood this, but he gave it little thought as he recovered from the first fight with Joe Frazier and began looking ahead to his next opponent. When you lose to the champion, you have to fight your way back into contention again. It would be three years before Ali would have another opportunity to box for the title.

By 1974, heavyweight boxing, largely through the efforts and charisma of Muhammad Ali, had become a strikingly glamorous affair. Movie stars and other celebrities regularly attended the fights. Closed-circuit theater broadcasts had made it possible for fighters to earn five million dollars in a night. But according to boxing folks in the know, no amount of money should have been enough to induce the aging Muhammad Ali to fight George Foreman, the reigning champion. Not only had Foreman beaten Joe Frazier, he had hammered and dazed him so thoroughly that the fight had to be stopped in the second round. And George Foreman had knocked out nearly everyone else he'd ever fought, too. Like Ali, he'd won an Olympic gold medal—but he'd won it eight years more recently than Ali. Their battle in Zaire, the so-called "Rumble in the Jungle," had all the makings of a terrible mismatch.

And when the fight began, that was what it looked

like. During the first round, Ali danced as he had in the old days, but it was obvious he couldn't do it for long. Angelo Dundee and the others in Ali's corner only hoped he could somehow stay away from young Foreman long enough to tire him out. Then maybe Ali would be able to wear him down further with punches. Maybe there'd be a chance. But the first part of the plan had to be "Dance for as long as you can."

Imagine the horror in Dundee's heart, then, when Ali stopped dancing toward the end of round one and leaned passively against the ropes. He watched as Foreman hesitated, then started throwing punches. Here was a heavyweight's dream: an apparently stationary target. Foreman launched an enormous left hook that would have ended the fight if it had connected, but it missed by six inches. He launched another one, and it missed, too. Dundee prayed for the bell to ring. It finally did, and each fighter returned to his corner.

"What are you doing?!" Dundee and the other corner men screamed at Ali. "Get off the ropes! Don't let him tee off on you that way! He'll kill you!"

Ali looked at them serenely, weirdly composed in the middle of the noise and excitement. He'd been fighting professionally for fourteen years, and he'd had hundreds of amateur bouts before he'd turned pro. He knew as well as anyone alive how alone a boxer is in the ring. A thousand people can shout advice. Ten million can cheer for you or roar for the other guy to knock your block off. But finally you find your own way in the ring, and Ali felt he'd intuitively discovered the way to beat the heavily favored Foreman.

For the next six rounds, eighteen eternal minutes,

Ali kept backing onto the ropes and covering up his face with his hands. Foreman obligingly trudged after him, banging away at Ali's sides, his shoulders, his arms—any target Ali would present.

"What's happening?" somebody shouted at Dundee.

"I don't know," the trainer had to admit. He'd never seen anything like it. Ali seemed to be inviting the champion to beat him to pieces.

But suddenly, in the seventh round, Foreman began to appear exhausted. Norman Mailer, one of the writers attending the fight, later described him as looking like he was trying to climb a mountain of pillows. By round eight he had nothing left. Ali waited for him to throw a punch that would expose his head, and then, as if he'd been planning it for months, he knocked Foreman out.

Later that night it rained hard, the way it rains only in the tropics. A reporter named Pete Bonventre decided to try to visit the cottage where Muhammad Ali was staying to see if he could get a post-fight comment or two. The rain had kept the other writers away, and when Bonventre finally made it to Ali's porch, he found him on the steps. "Three hours after the greatest victory of his life," the reporter recalls, "Muhammad Ali was sitting on the stoop, showing a magic trick to a group of black children. It was a rope trick, where the rope is cut in half and then it's suddenly back together again. And it was hard to tell who was having the better time, Ali or the children. All I could think was, I don't care what anyone says, there'll never be anyone like him again."

Muhammad Ali did not retire, even after reclaiming the title. As a young man he had beaten Sonny Liston, who had seemed so much stronger and tougher. As an old man, at least in boxing terms, he had beaten Foreman, who was young as Ali had once been. He went on to fight for five more years. He ignored the evidence of his own deterioration and the pleading of his fans, his family, and his doctor. He lost the title to Leon Spinks, then won it back again. Nobody had ever reclaimed the heavyweight title that many times.

But Muhammad Ali took several fearsome beatings. He began to suffer from a condition called Parkinson's syndrome. After he finally did retire, he often appeared tired and awkward, which was sad for people who had watched him dance in the ring. He often had difficulty speaking clearly, which was sad for the people who had heard him talk with such wit and fire and conviction.

Boxing damages everyone it touches, and it has damaged Muhammad Ali. But he still prays five times each day. He still travels all over the world, urging people to live in peace. And he still represents for countless people, whether they like boxing or not, an embodiment of courage.

To the Field Goal Kicker in a Slump

by Linda Pastan

*Even great athletes know what it feels like
to fail in a key situation. The speaker of
this poem explores the frustrations of an
athlete who fails again and again.*

It must be something
like writer's block,
when nothing will go
between the margins,
5   when language won't soar
high enough,
when you wake
in the morning and know
you've chosen
10   the wrong game.

Acknowledgments

Continued from page ii

Rina Ferrarelli: "Joan Benoit: 1984 U.S. Olympic Marathon Gold Medalist" by Rina Ferrarelli. Reprinted by permission of the author.

Little, Brown and Company: "Muhammad Ali," from *Champions* by Bill Littlefield. Text Copyright © 1993 by Bill Littlefield. Illustrations Copyright © 1993 by Bernie Fuchs. By permission of Little, Brown and Company.

W. W. Norton & Company, Inc.: "To a Field Goal Kicker in a Slump," from *A Fraction of Darkness* by Linda Pastan. Copyright © 1985 by Linda Pastan. Reprinted by permission of W. W. Norton & Company, Inc.